The Holy Grail

THE HOLY GRAIL

The Legend, the History, the Evidence

by

Justin Griffin

McFarland & Company, Inc., Publishers
Jefferson, North Carolina, and London

Library of Congress Cataloguing-in-Publication Data

Justin, Griffin.
    The Holy Grail : the legend, the history, the evidence / by
Justin Griffin.
        p.   cm.
    Includes bibliographical references and index.
    ISBN 0-7864-0999-1 (softcover : 60# alkaline paper) ∞
    1. Grail—Legends—History and criticism.   2. Grail.
I. Title.
PN686.G7G75   2001
398'.35—dc21   2001031219

British Library cataloguing data are available

Manufactured in the United States of America

Cover image ©2001 PhotoSpin

*McFarland & Company, Inc., Publishers
    Box 611, Jefferson, North Carolina 28640
    www.mcfarlandpub.com*

To my wife, Donna Griffin,
whose love, dedication, encouragement, and
perseverance made this book come to fruition.

Also to my mother, Peggy Griffin,
with love and thanks.

Acknowledgments

When I began researching the Grail legend about six years ago, I had no idea where it would lead me or what I was about to get myself into. I just started reading.

Once I felt I had enough knowledge to begin discussing the legend, I began an Internet web site and discussion group about my thoughts and findings. This allowed me the opportunity to speak with a widely diverse group of people from all around the globe. As it turned out, having access to their knowledge and theories made all the difference.

I would like to thank all the people who contributed to the making of this book. First among them are the members, past and present, of the e-mail discussion group, the Grail Group. Among these, special thanks go out to John Koopmans, who contributed many of the pictures contained in this book, and Juan C. Gorostizaga, a good brother of the Cofradía del Santo Cáliz de Valencia, who introduced the Santo Cáliz and its history to me. A special thanks to Mr. Fernando Parrado of the University of Tennessee, Knoxville, who helped me translate the book Juan sent to me about the Santo Cáliz. My thanks also to Claudia Lüdtke, who took several pictures of the chapel of the Volto Santo in Lucca, Italy, and to Francis Thye, who contributed the picture of Saint Joseph's Well, as well as all the good people at Glastonbury Abbey who have been so helpful during my research.

Finally, my thanks to all those friends and family members who have had to read several iterations of this text before it was completed. Thank you Donna, Janet, Tim Watson, Ann Lacava, and Dr. Laura Howes.

CONTENTS

PREFACE

Why would someone choose to study a subject like the legend of the Holy Grail? Why not study some other, more tangible historical object or event? Why waste time trying to prove what must surely be a mere myth?

To me, the greatest part of the human character is the desire to know. This means not only knowing things that can be useful in everyday life, but also knowing things just for the sake of knowing. Humans have a capacity to look beyond the obvious and delve into questions that, while serving no physical purpose, tempt the mind to expand a bit—grow beyond the knowledge of science, government, and economics. Mysteries such as the Grail make man's walk through life interesting.

My interest in researching the Grail, along with other legends of early Christianity, began in 1993. I had always been interested in the legends of King Arthur and medieval history in general; then, my interest in ancient religious artifacts was piqued by a documentary discussing the historical evidence surrounding the Ark of the Covenant. The two interests combined led to one intriguing legend: that of the Holy Grail.

It astounded me that archeologists and other researchers had ever seriously pursued what I had thought was just myth and story. This made me wonder what hidden chambers and lost pathways might be found if I, too, investigated the texts and histories associated with the Grail legend. Thus began my own quest. Since I worked at a university library at the time, I had what I thought was a limitless supply of reference material with which I might feed my curiosity. However, I soon exhausted the resources at hand and began looking elsewhere for information. As I drew from sources made available to me though interlibrary loan, my notebooks filled a little more.

It was not until I began to tap the vast world of the Internet, and the contacts made via my Grail Legend website and discussion group, that I began to make any real, measurable advancement. Being exposed to literally a world full of other legends and histories allowed me to see the Grail legend in a whole new light. I began to believe it possible that a historical Grail may exist.

However, this new world of information presented problems. I soon found that there was so much information about the Grail, and that so much of it was contradictory, that it would be quite difficult to determine what information could be true and what false.

As luck would have it, this very conundrum would lead me to an important realization. In the midst of a sea of confusion, contradictory accounts of separate objects and histories, all having what seemed to be a valid claim to the title of "THE Holy Grail," I found that I had been looking at the problem all wrong.

Just as the Grail hero Perceval needed to ask the right question at the right time, I realized that I had been over-instructed on how to deal with the Grail. I needed to approach the mystery in bare ignorance, not clothed in the armor of preconceived notions. I realized that the only way to understand the Grail and its legend was to unlearn all I already thought I knew about the subject, and simply follow where the facts led. By this method, I discovered a path through the tangle of information. This book retraces that path.

The book outlines the basics of the Grail legend, investigates the historical aspects of events that led to the legend, and, finally, examines the legitimacy of the claims made by several contenders for the Holy Grail, concluding with a new theory about the mysterious artifact. Subjects covered in this book include the main body of the Grail legend, including the story of the life of Christ and His crucifixion, the secondary histories and legends associated with those who played a part in His burial, the medieval search for the Grail and other relics of the Passion, and the historical references pointing back to the Grail that have been hidden in time and lost in apathy.

The Grail legend is one of the best known stories to survive the Middle Ages, but it is also possibly the least understood. Most treatises dealing with the Grail incorrectly relegate it to the realm of Celtic folklore, Christianized to suit the proper audience, or else treat the Grail as a simple idea to be approached as a mere psychological or spiritual study. Few investigations deal with the Grail as an historical object, as real as a pot shard or the ruins of a city.

It is my hope that this book will lead its readers to the understanding that the truth is sometimes much stranger than fiction. Sometimes, the things we dismiss as common knowledge may reveal, on closer examination, elements of mystery and surprise.

1

BIBLICAL ORIGINS
OF THE GRAIL

Before beginning a discussion about the existence or nonexistence of the Holy Grail, it is first necessary to speak about the nature of myth and legend. When someone uses the word "legend," what is truly being said? The word holds a peculiar place in our vernacular. It is simultaneously fact and fiction, truth and fantasy. It cannot be dismissed as an utter fabrication, because the word contains a hint of truth. Nor can it be completely accepted as historical fact, because the word suggests an element of fantasy. Therefore, a researcher investigating a historical legend such as the Grail is in a peculiar position. The available information is usually less than reliable, and often there is so little information, reliable or not, that nothing new can be discovered.

Anyone in search of a real, historical Holy Grail must acknowledge these limitations. The search of the Grail is not a mathematical proof that can be verified, nor is it a chemical equation that follows a set path. It is an adventure into an unknown land where there are few rules and no trodden path to follow. There is simply a course in which one step seems to point to another, then another. The only guide one has on such a mission is the simplest logic and the lonely voice of reason. Understanding myth is an act of progression and regression ending in a simple, logical whole.

There are certain such myths that enchant the human mind — things that, although inherently irrational and fantastic, become part of our culture. The greatest character of the human heart is the desire to discover, especially if the discovery is truly the stuff of legends. Even now in a society of instantaneous telecommunications and the perilous realms of cyberspace, some things are so old, and so ingrained, they become like the earth itself—no one really questions, but simply assumes they've always been just as we now know them. Such things can also seem so accepted and well defined that most people believe a close examination is pointless. However, if history teaches anything, it is that no historical event is as simple as it seems, especially as its antiquity increases and the memory of the event diminishes.

The most deeply ingrained of our legends leave traces in our imagination, and these traces are illuminated whenever the mind encounters a riddle or a mystery. Such is the case with the legend of Arthur, the once king of Britain, and that of the enigmatic relic, the Holy Grail. Although it has become somewhat clichéd, the victim of too much Hollywood rough-handedness and modern retelling, the Grail remains one myth that fails to die with the passing of time. The lore may fade for a hundred years at a time, but the luminous, misty fog of the Grail's story always reappears, re-creating its own mythos, stirring and attracting the inquisitive mind.

The legend of King Arthur and the Grail may at first appear to be a fairly simple, purely fictional story. However, when beginning the task of researching these legends, it becomes all too clear that the defining boundaries of their parent texts are not so well defined as one might imagine. An inquisitive student may begin by peering into the heroic tales of Arthur and the veiled shores of Avalon, but very soon begins to track down information about a reference to something outside the text. Journeying down that separate path, the Grail student may find an entirely new, terribly complex realm of study awaiting investigation. In fact, the associated legends, histories, and texts are so numerous, and of such widely diverse origins, that a lifetime could easily be devoted to their study alone.

While the more popular of these legends is that of King Arthur and his exploits, the legend of the Holy Grail offers a more challenging wealth of historical study. It may be that people who are familiar with the Arthur legend are less acquainted, or even entirely unfamiliar, with the saga of the Grail. Therefore Grail researchers must begin their path of discovery by outlining the main points that form the structure of this age-draped mystery. Although there are literally dozens of different stories and texts, a devoted researcher finds that there are certain repeating themes, and familiar names and events, throughout. As the investigation progresses, it becomes clear why the Grail is the greatest mystery to emerge from the Middle Ages.

What is the Grail? This simple question holds the single most important truth enshrined in the Grail legend. It is the question that must be asked by those who seek the Grail, the question that will restore life to a king and abundance to his land, and the question that scholarly "Grail Questers" must endeavor to answer. However, to ask this is to question the true nature of humanity. Are we spiritual beings? Are we purely logical? Cynical? Gullible? To search for the Grail is not an activity to be lightly undertaken. One who makes the decision will be confronted with everything from thousand-year-old mysteries to the superstitions of all mankind.

Although the Grail is a Christian myth, to call it an entirely Christian legend is to misunderstand the whole nature of the Grail Quest. To fully understand the Grail's mystique, one must be versed in Celtic mythology, Persian history and literature, trade and commerce in the ancient world, European history, and most importantly, the characteristics of the human mind. Most modern studies of the Grail center either on its possible origins in Celtic myth, or the metaphysical aspects of the Quest. A hundred years ago, the Grail served as an icon for reclaiming the lost glory of the Holy Roman Empire. A thousand years ago, the Grail was no less than the essence of Jesus Christ Himself. However, these are not the analyses in which this study will be interested. What is truly important to consider is what the Grail was to a small group of Hebrews—a small group that would soon become the first Christians.

The Grail legend begins with a story of Christ's life and death. One very important aspect of the story is that it takes place in the shadow of Roman rule in Palestine. At the height of its power, the Roman Empire stretched across the known world from Britain to the Middle East. Although the Romans are usually considered to be ruthless conquerors, they more commonly expanded their empire through assimilation rather than domination. They quite often allowed the continuation of native customs and religious practice in the lands they seized, in the effort to reduce the possibility of insurrection.

Although Christian history remembers brutality and persecution at the hands of Roman rule, the Jewish culture was allowed to continue more or less as it was used to under their new authority. Therefore the crucifixion of Christ was not an act of domination over a religious minority. It was simply an act of capital punishment, carried out by Roman authorities as a political crime, backed by the claims of heresy by the Jewish leadership, the Sanhedrin. This idea is further proven when one researches the act of crucifixion during this period. This was not a punishment handed out to every offender. Although crucifixion was used occasionally as a visual warning to "make an example" of someone, it was most often used for the most heinous offenses, such as treason. These facts present a picture of Christ's death that demonstrate a rare, brutal fate—one that would be given to the most dangerous of all criminals at the time.

In the last year of His life, Jesus Christ entered the city of Jerusalem in Palestine around the time of Passover. He and His disciples had spread His ministry across the land until it became a threat to the traditions and power of the existing religious leaders, the Sanhedrin. Although a Jew himself, Christ's teachings went against many basic, fundamental edicts of the Jewish faith, quickly causing Him to be viewed as a danger that had to be managed. Knowing this, Christ gathered his disciples together and held what is now referred to as "The Last Supper," the traditional meal of Passover.

Even as the plan to arrest Him was taking place, Christ transformed a traditional Jewish tradition into one of the most important events in the Christian faith. In the pouring of wine and the breaking of bread, He told His disciples that they were to take these elements and consume them, for the bread was His body, and the wine was His blood—a tradition to be maintained even in His impending absence. He told them that He was soon to leave them and that they were to hold this "Lord's Supper," later to be called the Eucharist, in remembrance of Him.

Soon afterward, Judas, one of Jesus's own followers, betrayed Him and turned Him over to the soldiers of the Roman magistrate Pontius Pilate. He was charged both socially and politically, being accused of heresy by the Sanhedrin for calling Himself the Son of God, and of treason against Rome by calling Himself the King of the Jews. In the following days, Christ was nailed to a cross He had dragged along the Via Dolorosa to the hill of Golgotha. There He hung crucified until the Roman centurion, Longinus, pierced His side with a spear to ensure His death, thus fulfilling the prophecy that not one bone of the Messiah's body would be broken.

After Christ's death, Joseph of Arimathea, a wealthy Jew of some social standing and importance, went to Pilate and requested the crucified body. Joseph took it and placed it in his own finely prepared tomb, wrapped in his own rich burial cloth, and, according to Grail legend, collected a small amount of Christ's blood in the Grail during the preparation of His body for interment. Two days later, the stone door to the tomb was found rolled away from the opening, revealing an empty tomb.

Today, the time from Christ's entrance into Jerusalem, through His Passion, to the discovery of His empty tomb, is called the "Holy Week." This week ending with the Easter holiday is considered to be the most revered period in the Christian year, even more so than Christmas. The following is a timeline outlining the most significant events recognized during Holy Week. (Note: the timeline listed below is according to our system of days, not the Jewish calendar. The Jewish "day" ends at sundown, so Thursday night, the night of the Last Supper, would have been considered Friday—thus the statement that Jesus rose from the tomb on "the third day.")

Sunday:	(One week before Easter) Christ entered Jerusalem.
Monday:	Jesus overthrew the money-changers' tables in the temple.
Tuesday:	Preached to the people of Jerusalem.
Wednesday:	Preached to the people of Jerusalem. Most probable time of Jesus attending the dinner in His honor at the house of Martha and Mary, when Mary anointed Christ's feet or head with Nard.
Thursday:	The Last Supper, institution of the New Covenant; the betrayal by Judas.
Friday:	Christ's arrest in the Garden of Gethsemane; trial before Pilate, crucifixion, death, and burial in the new tomb.
Saturday:	(Jewish Sabbath) Christ rested in the tomb.
Sunday:	Christ's tomb is found empty.

With the exception of Joseph collecting Christ's blood in some kind of container, the preceding story is taken directly from the four Gospels as found in the New Testament of the Bible. This story is familiar to and indeed sacred among Christians and does not easily accept addition or alteration. However, even those same Christians will agree that the Bible is not meant to be an all-inclusive history book for that time. The Bible tells the story of its characters, and the story of

Christ tells about His life and His death. Later events, including the travels of the Apostles and the evolution of Christianity, are more the subject of history books.

In the tumultuous time to follow, history and legend would blur, and traditions would change rapidly. Christianity would be persecuted by Rome, then adopted as the national religion. Under the first Christian Roman Emperor, Constantine, and thanks largely to his mother Helena, there would be a time of incredible, intense interest in "holiness," especially holy sites and objects. Helena's travels to Jerusalem resulted in the construction of the magnificent Church of the Holy Sepulchre in Jerusalem, built on the site where she found Christ's tomb. However, the years to follow would bring the most important event in the history of the ancient world—the fall of the Roman Empire. This slow dissolution would spawn a great era of mystery and confusion known as the Dark Ages from which would come the legend of King Arthur and later that of the Holy Grail.

From here, one must embark on a study of the legendary King Arthur, the semimythical king of ancient Britain. The earliest mentions of Arthur were made by Nennius and the Venerable Bede. However, he first appears in literature in the Welsh tale of *Culhwch and Olwen* where the Welsh prince Culhwch asks the assistance of King Arthur to win the affection of Olwen, a giant's daughter. The early picture of Arthur is what one would expect of a fifth-century Romano-Celtic warrior chieftain. Then, in Wace's *Roman de Brut*, we are told a more courtly and historically rooted story of Arthur's rise to kingship.

After the withdrawal of the Roman presence in Britain, a warlord named Vortigern allied himself with the invading Saxons. Two brothers named Ambrosius and Uther, who had been exiled from Britain when Vortigern killed the previous king Constance, then returned to Britain to combat Vortigern and his Saxon allies. This rivalry was pictured in the famous tale of Merlin's discovery of the red dragon and white dragon sleeping in a subterranean lake under Vortigern's castle that would collapse despite every effort to keep the walls standing. Merlin stated that as long as these dragons warred, Vortigern would never rule over the lands of Britain. Furthermore, Merlin told Vortigern to beware the brothers Ambrosius and Uther, for they represented the red dragon who would soon overcome his white dragon, driving Vortigern forever from the land.

The prophecy soon came true when Ambrosius became king of Britain. However, Ambrosius would soon die from poisoning, leaving the kingship to Uther, now called the Pendragon (the Head Dragon). Seeking to be the one and only king of all Britain, Uther wars with the Duke of Cornwall. Upon seeing the beauty of the Duke's wife Igraine, Uther becomes determined to have her as his own wife, regardless of the consequences. With the assistance of Merlin the magician, he steals into the Duke's castle, and magically takes the appearance of the Duke, tricking Igraine into thinking he is her husband. While Uther spends the night in Igraine's bed, the real Duke of Cornwall is killed. After that night, it is discovered that Igraine is pregnant with a child that could only have been fathered by Uther.

This child named Arthur is taken by Merlin to be raised by a noble knight named Sir Ector, and he is trained to be a squire to his foster brother, Sir Kei. Some years later, when Arthur is a young man, his brother is to take part in a tournament of arms. Upon finding his brother's sword missing, Arthur sets out looking for a replacement, as he has been taught to do as his brother knight's squire. In his searching he happens across a magnificent sword embedded in a stone. He carefully places his hands upon it to recover it for Kei, but try as he might, the sword will not budge. Angrier and angrier he becomes, desperate to do his duty.

Upon the scene strides an old man who instructs him to be calm, and to expect the sword to release itself from the stone. Doing as the old man suggested, Arthur calmly pulled upward on the handle of this magical sword, and slid it cleanly from the rock. The other knights from the tournament then arrived at the sacred stone to behold this holy indicator that this boy, Arthur, was to be their one true king.

As time passed, Arthur brought together the lands of Britain, bringing a golden time of peace and plenty over his kingdom. However, as the medieval concept of the Wheel of Fortune dictates, this golden age could last only for a time. The years of wealth and ease soon left King Arthur and his knights complacent in their knightly roles. Then, during the feast at Pentecost, the entire court was brought to a state of holy wonderment by an object that illuminated the room and came to rest, hovering over the table. After some time, the radiant object vanished, leaving all present in a state of awe. It was explained that this object was the Holy Grail. Thereafter, in a renewed state of vigor, the knights dedicated their lives to finding and worshipping this object. The Quest had begun.

Only three of these knights, Bors, Perceval, and the perfect, virgin knight Galahad, were successful in drawing near to the Grail since the others were too full of worldly vices. Of these, only Galahad is allowed to touch the Grail. Earlier in the story, he sits in the "Siege Perilous," the thirteenth seat at the round table that swallows up everyone else who attempts to sit there. By doing this he is proven to be the only one pure enough of heart to attain the Grail.

According to the legend, the Grail was taken by Joseph of Arimathea from Jerusalem to Britain after Christ's crucifixion. Accompanied by a small group of followers, including his daughter and her husband Bron (or Bran), they formed a holy community, initiating the sacrament of communion using the Grail, the cup used by Christ at the Last Supper, and used to collect some of His blood as the body was taken down from the Cross. Fed by the spirit of God descending as a white dove filling the cup with the Host (the body of Christ), this "Grail family" guards the relic that is passed down to Bron, who comes to be known as the Rich Fisher King. Bron, himself mortally wounded but unable to die, guards the Grail until Galahad arrives to complete his quest, thus releasing the Fisher King to his death, and restoring order to the realm.

The legends of King Arthur permeated the entirety of medieval life and beyond. Throughout the Middle Ages, King Arthur was used to validate succession of power, the overthrow of rulers, and to manufacture associated legends. Arthurian legend can be traced, in one form or another, all the way back to Celtic mythology. Kings of England claimed to possess items associated with Arthur, such as the sheath to Excalibur, the bridle and reins for his horse, even books allegedly written by the legendary king. Then, when the legend of the Grail became associated with King Arthur in popular culture, interest in the search for the historical King Arthur was reborn with a renewed vigor.

The Grail legend had a more personal impact on medieval culture than did the Arthur legend. While Arthur was well known at the time, every Christian soul felt a certain amount of connection to the Grail. In the Roman Catholic Church, the items of the Eucharist were usually kept hidden from the masses of devotees present during the service. However, when these items were uncovered for all to see, it began the feeling of a real, material closeness to Christ. Therefore, the Grail and the Grail Quest symbolized the perfect search for Christ—the attempt to touch something, to touch a physical object that had once been touched by Jesus Himself. While this explains the popularity of these tales, this does not relegate the Grail legend to pure fiction.

The most well-known version of the Grail Quest is mostly that found in Sir Thomas Malory's *Le Morte Darthur*, written in the fifteenth century. However, this is a relatively recent work about Arthur and the Grail, stemming from earlier works, most notably those of Chrétien de Troyes and Robert de Boron. It is curious to note that the hero of these early works was not Galahad, the flawless, virgin knight, but rather Perceval, described as "the Perfect Fool," a simple Welsh boy who was purposely not educated as a knight.

Why then do these two versions of the same tale vary so greatly? Why do all the originating tales show Perceval as the hero instead of this relative newcomer, Galahad? Further, how could three generations of people live the several hundred years that span the time between Christ's crucifixion around AD 35 and the fifth or sixth century AD? Isn't the only logical conclusion that the entire tale of King Arthur and the Grail is simply a fanciful creation of a medieval bard or scribe, made for the amusement of his benefactor's court? Perhaps not. In fact, recent years have produced evidence that many aspects of the Arthurian legend were true, if not as magical as described in the medieval romances. Might it not therefore be possible that some aspects of the Grail legend are similarly historical and indeed true? The evidence for this hypothesis is compelling, although not undeniable. Judging by the facts found throughout the remainder of this book, it may even turn out that, not only is the Grail a true object, but that the true Holy Grail may turn out to be stranger than that of fiction.

2

EXAMINING THE
GRAIL TEXTS

When one begins researching the story of Arthur and the Grail, it is impossible to fully comprehend the depth of the world in which you are about to immerse yourself. Many begin their search expecting to glean all the answers needed from Malory's simple story. However, as the researcher strays from that text in order to research some "minor point," an entirely different arena of history is found.

All it takes is reading one modern treatment of the Grail legend to come to this realization. For example, the simple mention of the Knights Templar can lead a future Grail researcher into an incredibly complex study of medieval politics, religion, magic, heresies, and centuries of uncertain allegations. It then becomes all too clear that the story of the Grail is not quite as cut and dried as it would seem. Then, after reading these modern theses on the Grail legend's history, one might assume that the answer to "What is the Grail?" has been found. However, the discovery of a small reference or simply an overlooked fact can completely destroy all previously held assumptions.

The most important thing to remember when embarking on the quest for answers about the Holy Grail, or about any legendary topic, is expect to be led 'round the garden path, so to speak. There are as many different facets in each tale as there have been people telling it, trying to put their own agendas forward, and trying to please their own patrons. However, if one has a good sense of human nature and a close eye for detail, it soon becomes clear what to weed out and what to file away for future reference. To begin the weeding-out process, it is necessary to refer to the originating texts and to see what the earliest reference to the Grail might be.

The story of Arthur, the king of Britain, began somewhere in the fifth or sixth century AD. Many have heard the legend, but how much of this is historical fact? In this case, there is actually some evidence to fall back on in the search. According to archeological and historical data, Arthur was a Romano-Celtic warrior chieftain who won several key battles against the Saxons.

Britain was controlled by the Roman Empire as far north as Hadrian's Wall until just before the time of Arthur. Roman influence is still quite easy to see throughout England in the architecture of Roman aqueducts and communal bath houses. To more easily maintain their rule, the Romans employed local Celtic tribal lords to serve as "vassals" over their remote lands. After the withdrawal of the Roman forces, Britain experienced a type of power vacuum, causing these overlords and chieftains to war amongst themselves for control of their homelands. Ironically, the most powerful leaders during this time were those who could claim to be descended of Roman blood.

Among these leaders one fairly successful warrior is mentioned, variously named "Artu" and "Artos," who would later be known by his Latinized name, "Artorius" or Arthur. In fact, a stone bearing the engraved name of "Artgonou" was discovered in the late 1990s around the Cornwall region, demonstrating how widespread the name of "Arthur" was after his time. The Welsh monk Nennius stated in his *Historia Brittonum*, written around the year AD 830, that Arthur was instrumental in turning back the Anglo-Saxons at the battle of Badon which, according to Bede's eighth century *Ecclesiastical History of the English People*, took place in AD 493. The Battle of Badon is also recorded in *On the Ruin and Conquest of Britain*, written by the British monk Gildas around AD 545. Here it is clear to see that someone with a name like "Arthur" was a noteworthy British military figure around the turn of the fifth century.

Although it appears that Arthur was a historical figure, it may be that he is not simply one person. The reason why there is separate, conflicting evidence regarding who the historical King Arthur is may be answered in Adrian Gilbert's book, *The Holy Kingdom*. This book presents evidence that the King Arthur of legend was actually two different Arthurs. These two Welsh kings were Arthur I who is named

Andragathius, or Arthun, the son of Magnus Maximus, the alleged grandson of Constantine the Great; and secondly, the Arthur who fought the Saxons at the battle of Badon in the sixth century, Arthur II named Athrwys, the son of Meurig. According to this theory, Arthur I was buried near Atherstone in Warwickshire, while Arthur II was buried at the Church of St. Peter's in the Upper Ewenny area.

This book makes another interesting assertion relating to Empress Helena and her visit to Jerusalem in the fourth century. When Helena found the tomb of Christ, she allegedly found several objects used during the crucifixion inside the tomb, including the cross of the crucifixion. The legend states that pieces of the cross and the nails that accompanied it were sent to her son, Constantine the Great. However, *The Holy Kingdom* states that the cross did not finish its travels at this point.

> What seems to have happened is that Helen paraded the Cross around the country on a grand tour, before depositing it in its final resting place for safekeeping. The route that she followed then became a sort of "pilgrim's way." It is significant that one can today go along these roads following a route marked by Cross names. There is "the Pass of the Cross," "the Mountain of the Cross," "the Valley of the Cross," "the Ford of the Cross," "the Vale of the Cross," "the Fields of the Cross" and so on. The final destination of the Cross is recorded in the king lists drawn up for the wedding of Owen, the son of Hywell Dda (Howell the Good) of Dyfed— part of the Harleian 3859 collection of manuscripts. This collection is a most important corpus of texts concerning Wales and the Dark Ages. The king lists are contained in the famous "Black Book of Carmarthen," and were drawn up to demonstrate his descent from a number of intermarried royal houses. Surprising as it may seem, it states clearly that at the time of writing, around 920, the Cross was in Dyfed in south-west Wales [Gilbert, pp. 141–142].

Evidence to support the idea of the cross being in Wales can be found in a rock cliff at Nevern. Taking a path down the side of the cliff, there is a place where the Christian faithful have visited on pilgrimage for centuries. The Pilgrim's Cross of Nevern is a curious carving of a cross on the cliff wall with a small step or pedestal beneath it on which people may kneel and pray before the carving. At first glance, this carving appears fairly normal, despite its precarious location. However, a close inspection reveals an intriguing, apparently hidden feature. Only the upper portion of the cross is actually sculpted from the rock of the cliff side, while the lower portion is crafted from separate stones, fitted

The Pilgrim's Cross of Nevern (John Koopmans).

into place, and disguised to look like the natural rock. It is theorized that the cross taken to Wales by Helena is hidden behind this wall.

It would seem a simple matter to deconstruct the wall and see if this theory is correct. However, this site is seen as a national protected site, guarded against desecration. Despite this protected status, a visitor to the site carefully removed a brick from the wall and indeed found a cavity or passageway behind the fake wall. It is postulated that behind this façade, there is another wall or structure, possibly from an earlier date, that once or possibly still does contain the cross on which Christ was crucified.

It appears that not only was King Arthur an historical figure, he may have been two different people whose legacy has been intertwined over the passing of time. Furthermore, the Pilgrim's Cross of Nevern demonstrates that Empress Helena and relics of the Passion appear to have visited Wales at some point. For these reasons, the legend of Arthur and the accounts of relics in Britain would seem historical. Therefore the question must be asked—if Arthur was a historical figure, what about the rest of the story? Were the Round Table, its knights, Excalibur, Camelot, Avalon, and the Grail real as well?

While many of these more familiar aspects of the Arthur legend were created purely for the flow of the medieval tales, they may lead to a bit of history as well. For example, the Grail legend states that the famous Round Table of Arthur's court was simply the last of three famous tables—first, the table of the Last Supper, at which Christ and His twelve disciples sat, accompanied by Judas in the thirteenth seat; second, the table of the Rich Fisher King, with a fish placed at the thirteenth seat to represent the absent Christ; and third, the Round Table of Arthur, the thirteenth seat now called the Siege Perilous, representing the place once occupied by Judas, in which could sit only the most perfect, pure knight in all the world—Galahad.

Historically speaking, there is little evidence to support the existence of such a table. The only real manifestation of it can be found in the Great Hall of Winchester Castle in the form of a five-meter reproduction built for King Henry III in the thirteenth century. As there was never any other artifact discovered, this table is considered to be a commemoration of the Arthur legend and its Round Table.

The knights of the Round Table were also more fictional than historical. With the exception of Gawain and Perceval, the most famous knights such as Lancelot, Bors, and Galahad appear to have either been heroes of other earlier tales or archetypal "heroes" created to suit the

The round table at Winchester Castle (John Koopmans).

story. Although some of these names can be found in other spheres of pseudohistory, the nature of Arthur's court is rather vague, since the number of the Round Table knights varied greatly from 12 or 13 to well over 100.

The nature of Excalibur, Camelot, and Avalon are somewhat more difficult to pin down. Dismissing the magical myths attributed to each, these are aspects of the Arthur legend which may have had factual origins. The hero's sword, be it Excalibur, The sword of Roland, or the sword of Beowulf, has been a repeating symbol of divine justice objectified long before medieval times. Excalibur may have been simply a device used to display Arthur's divine right as King of Britain (especially in light of the ritual liberation of the sword from the unyielding stone). On the other hand, it may have been an actual object, used by Arthur during his battles, which has been magnified and exaggerated over time. Such was the case concerning the famous story of Charlemagne, who wished to demonstrate that his power was greater than that of the Church by taking the crown of kingship from the Pope and placing it on his head himself. Graham Phillips, in his book *The Search for the Grail*, makes the assertion that the sword may have been the symbol of Roman imperial authority. This theory gains credibility when we discover from Roman texts that leadership rights in Roman Britain were settled in single combat, the victor drawing a "sword of office" from a stone.

Camelot, the seat of Arthur's court, has been placed at several different locations in Britain including Tintagel, Glastonbury, locations in Wales, and Bath. Phillips presents a theory stating that Camelot, in the fifth century Romano-Celtic sense, was found in the Welsh Kingdom of Powys. He claims that just before the withdrawal of Roman legions from the Isle of Britain, the city of Virconium underwent a dramatic renovation. His assertion is that Arthur, here identified as Owain Ddantgwyn, was the ruler of Virconium, or Powys, around the middle of the fifth century. Although the evidence Phillips cites is compelling, archeological evidence suggests that the site of Cadbury hill in Somerset is the most likely candidate for the historical Camelot. Excavations have determined a history of military fortifications on the site dating back to the Bronze Age. Although many other researchers have their own opinions as to where Arthur's golden citadel may have been, most that care to pick a site as the most probable location for Avalon choose the site at Cadbury.

Although the most popular account of Arthur, Avalon, and the Grail is Sir Thomas Malory's *Le Morte Darthur*, the earliest western mention of the Grail in literature is with *Le Conte du Graal.* This text, the work of French cleric Chrétien de Troyes, was the last of his Arthurian works, and was unfinished at the time of his death. According to Chrétien, the poem he wrote was simply a retelling of a story found in a book given to him by Prince Phillip of Flanders (a retelling which Price Phillip said must be given the greatest diligence). In this text, the Grail hero is Perceval, a Welsh youth who, while skilled in the use of a javelin, was untrained in the arts of knighthood. This was no accident. His mother kept Perceval from learning about knighthood because his father and uncles had all been killed in battle seeking chivalric deeds and glory. She kept him in the forest, taught him about Christianity, and instructed him on the recognition of angels and demons.

One day, while out in the woods throwing his javelin, he sees a band of luminous figures riding through the forest. First he thinks them to be angels, but remembers how his mother told him that evil spirits could also take pleasing shapes. His curiosity getting the better of him, he ventures forth and begins to ask the knights about themselves and their equipment. This encounter results in Perceval demanding to leave his mother to become a knight. Dressed in the finest Welsh attire, and instructed briefly in the ways of knighthood, Perceval journeys to the court of King Arthur to gain his knightly status. He is told he must first defeat the Red Knight and claim his armor to truly become a knight, which he soon does.

He later finds himself at the castle of the Rich Fisher King, after encountering the King in a fishing boat on a river outside the castle. Upon entering the castle, he is led to a banquet hall where he meets the Fisher King and sits down with him for a feast. During the meal, Perceval witnesses a procession in which several holy objects appear, among which is the Grail. He is stricken with awe upon seeing this and is moved to inquire as to its meaning. However, an old knight during his journeys warned him not to appear ignorant or irritating by asking too many questions, and to remain quiet. Therefore, despite his wonder, Perceval does not ask about the Grail or the procession even though it passes by him three times.

The next morning he rises and finds himself alone in the castle. He then replaces his armor and rides into the nearby forest. Almost immediately, a cloud forms and begins to rain over him, while a person walking on the other side of the stream remains dry. Perceval asks this person why only he is under the cloud. He is then told that, because he did not ask what was the Grail and who it serves, the King and his wasteland kingdom are doomed to remain in a state of misery between life and death—caused by the King's loss of faith.

Here is the crux of the Grail story. A king is mortally wounded but unable to die, languishing due to some sin of commission or omission, able to be released from his suffering by the arrival of one perfect knight who asks the vital question about the Grail. When that knight arrives and does not ask the question, his name becomes the object of ridicule and scorn. To redeem himself, he travels throughout the realm, performing many acts of bravery and valor, learning more of the Grail and the curious things he encounters along his travels, usually with the aid of a holy hermit living deep in the woods. Quite often these hermits were themselves knights who put down their arms in favor of a life of Christian devotion—a theme found throughout the Grail texts.

Why was this story written, and what meaning did it have? Was it simply a fanciful tale of mysticism and knightly bravery created to amuse the king and his court? Was there any kernel of truth to this story that has become legend? To discover this, it is necessary to learn more about Chrétien de Troyes and to examine the circumstances surrounding his most mysterious work.

Chrétien was born around 1135 in the town of Troyes in the Champagne region of France. Under the patronage of Countess Mary of Champagne, wife of Prince Henry of Champagne, and daughter of Louis VII and Eleanor of Aquitaine, his career hit its height between 1160 and 1180 when he wrote his other famous works, *Philomena*, *Erec and Enide*, *Cligès*, and his story of Lancelot and Guinevere, *Lancelot; or, The Knight of the Cart*. However the work in question, *Le Conte du Graal*, or *The Story of the Grail*, was written under the patronage of Prince Phillip of Flanders after the death of Prince Henry in 1181 one week after his return from the Holy Land. Soon after Henry's death, Prince Phillip intended to marry Countess Mary, who had retired to solitude, but the marriage never occurred. In 1190, he journeyed to the Holy Land during the Third Crusade, and died there of the plague one year later.

According to Chrétien's prologue to *The Story of the Grail*, in which he dedicates the work to Prince Phillip, a book containing the story of the Grail was actually given to him by Phillip. Chrétien was told to reproduce the story in verse and to give it his complete dedication. Although this tale was Chrétien's longest, most involved romance, he was unable to complete it before he died. It has always been a question who these continuators were, as most of their works remained anonymous.

However, reading the last paragraph of Chrétien's *The Knight of the Cart*, one possibility is presented.

> My lords, if I were to tell any more, I would be going beyond my matter. Therefore I draw to a close: the romance is completely finished at this point. The clerk Godefroy of Lagny has put the final touches on *The Knight of the Cart*; let no one blame him for completing the work of Chrétien, since he did it with the approval of Chrétien, who began it. He worked on the story from the point at which Lancelot was walled into the tower until the end. This much only has he done. He wishes to add nothing further, nor to omit anything, for this would harm the story. Here ends the romance of *Lancelot of the Cart* [Wilhelm, pp. 198–199].

Written around 1190, it was the first of several texts written in the following 30 years dealing with the Grail and Perceval's quest. These other texts, usually referred to as "The Continuations," included other important Grail texts such as two anonymous continuations written around 1195: Robert de Boron's text, *Joseph d'Arimathie* (the first work to place Joseph of Arimathea in the Grail legend outside the Bible), and the Didot Perceval, both written around 1200; *Parzifal*, written by Wolfram von Eschenbach in 1205; the anonymous work *Perlesvaus*, and the two stories of the *Vulgate Cycle*, written around 1220.

Although these are the most well-known texts in the Grail legend's reading list, they are by no means the only ones. Phillips makes reference to a work named *Fulke le Fitz Waryn*, which seems to have been derived, at least in part, from an earlier Welsh poem called the *Peveril*, written around 1100. It is theorized that this work was written by a late eleventh-century monk named Blayse of the abbey of St. Asaph in north Wales. This theory gains credibility when one recalls the statement made in the *Didot Perceval* that claims the original Grail story was taken from a book in the British language which was dictated to Brother Blayse.

The story of Blayse being dictated the story of Arthur and the Grail is reiterated not once, but four separate times in the *Prose Merlin* written in the thirteenth century. This story tells that Blayse was the confessor to Merlin's mother, and was also the person to whom Merlin repeated the story of his birth and the events of his life. "Merlin then went to join Blaise in Northumberland and related everything that had happened. Blaise put it into writing, and thanks to his book we know it today" (Wilhelm, p. 325).

However, the most important text regarding the Grail is found well outside these standard Grail texts. In 22 books entitled *Materials for History* covering the years between AD 407 and 425, the fifth-century Greek historian Olympiodorus recounts the story of Empress Helena discovering Christ's tomb that contained certain relics. One of these relics is mentioned as the "Marian Chalice," a vessel which Helena had reason to believe once contained the blood of Christ. From this historical reference, it is clear to see that although Chrétien was given credit for the first Grail text in Europe, it was not the first reference to the Grail.

With all these separate Grail texts, the existence of the Grail should be reinforced and verified. However, the unfortunate truth of old texts and ancient legends is that the greater the number of reference sources, the more confused the subject becomes. In fact with each text the true nature of the Grail becomes more obscure, becoming almost as many different things as there are versions of the story.

The best illustration of this problem can be found by reading the Celtic Arthurian and Grail texts which some claim are much older than Chrétien's work, or even possibly older than Christianity itself. If one has some knowledge of Celtic tradition, an examination of the original Grail texts reveals particular themes that one would not expect to find in a Christian tale.

With features of the Arthur/Grail myth such as the Lady of the Lake, the mention of Avalon, and the possession of a magical vessel, it is easy to assume that the entire Grail legend is an artifice of Celtic tradition, slightly altered into a story of Christian devotion. In fact, most scholars agree that Chrétien's original Grail text was a nearly exact re-creation of *Peredur*, taken from the Welsh *Mabinogion*.

The similarities are uncanny, with the exception of the object identified as the Grail. In *Peredur*, the Grail is a large, shallow bowl containing a severed but animate head resting in a pool of blood. This head is seen as an oracle, identifying it as an image of Celtic head worship. Archeological evidence supports the theory that the Celts worshiped the heads both of past leaders and powerful enemies. Many dwellings, sacred sites and lodges have been excavated that display human skulls built into the walls, placed in these strategic locations to ward off evil spirits and to serve as a warning to future enemies. Similarly, the enigmatic figure of the Fisher King appears to be of Celtic origin. The name given to him in some texts, Bron, is very similar to Bran, a character in ancient Celtic legend.

The Celtic relationship becomes more evident in the character of the Lady of the Lake. There is a great Celtic tradition in which maidens or water fairies are the guardians of cool, underground streams that lead to the Underworld. Here we see a close correlation to the Maiden of the Lake, the keeper of the magical sword Excalibur, and the water nymphs who, being supernatural beings themselves, are the keepers of the path into the realm of magic. Phillips provides historical evidence to this effect, speaking of the numerous "sacrificial offering" artifacts found while excavating the now-dry Llyn Cerrig Bach lake bed.

> The theme of Excalibur being thrown to the Lady of the Lake may therefore have derived from this ancient Celtic practice of making a sacred offering to a water goddess, perhaps from the notion that such an offering might restore the king to health. This hypothesis is further substantiated in the medieval romances, where the Lady of the Lake is given the name Viviane. This name could well have been an adaptation of Covianna, a Celtic water goddess recorded by Roman writers [Phillips, p. 8].

This theme is continued at the time of Arthur's death. After Excalibur is returned to the Lady of the Lake, Arthur is taken upon a radiant barge across the waters to the mystic Isle of Avalon. Now identified with Glastonbury, which would have been an island or a jutting peninsula amid the otherwise swampy marsh in the time of Arthur, Avalon is widely agreed to be a derivation of the Celtic word for the Underworld, Avaron. So what then does this examination demonstrate about the Grail? Is it too a Celtic creation?

Returning to the tale of *Peredur*, the Grail is seen as some sort of magic talisman, varying greatly from the object of Christian reverence. What does history tell us about a possible Celtic Grail? Archeology of the Celtic culture has demonstrated that cauldrons were revered, almost sacred objects. They were plentiful, ornate in many cases, and usually found in relation to the Celtic religion both in artwork and in physical location. This is supported by two other versions of the Arthurian tale called *The Spoils of Annwn* and *Culhwch and Olwen*, in which the King and his knights are questing for a magical cauldron exhibiting many of the same properties as the Grail in the traditional texts.

Throughout their mythology system, the Celts referred to magic cauldrons—great vessels which formed mankind, magic brews which renew life to fallen warriors, cornucopia-like cauldrons which give to a warrior a plentiful measure of his most desired food or drink, and the list goes on. In the anonymous First Continuation of Chrétien's originating Grail text, Gawain witnesses the Grail enter the hall in which he and the Rich Fisher King are dining and proceed to fill the plates and cups of the knights present. The likeness is made even more evident with the statement from the First Continuation that, "...Sir Gawain watched this, and marveled how much the Grail served them." This passage is clearly reminiscent of the Celtic cauldron of plenty: a vessel that provides as much good food and drink as each warrior (or knight) desires.

One fine example of extant Celtic vessels or cauldrons that may be potential contenders for the historical Grail is the Ardagh Chalice. This cup displays the fine craftsmanship and detail that would far exceed the quality of simple, utilitarian objects. It is not difficult to see this item as an object of Celtic holy worship, making it their version, and possibly the original version, of the Holy Grail.

In light of the obvious importance of the cauldron in Celtic religion and mythology, we must ask the question, is the legend of the Grail simply a Celtic myth taken from a pre-Christian culture and altered to suit the predominant society of the time? Can it be that simple? The answer is no. It is clearly not that simple. In fact, there is a preponderance of evidence which would lead to the belief that it is not of Celtic origin at all. Although the *Mabinogion* contains Celtic oral myths possibly originating from pre-Christian times, it is informally divided into two parts. The first four stories, Pwyll, Branwen, Manawydan, and Math, are probably at least several hundred years older than the date of AD 1325 when the *Mabinogion* was written. However, it is debated whether the last three books are that old.

The *Mabinogion* is simply a compilation of several Celtic oral traditions—an anthology of sorts. This means that the later books, including *Peredur*, are not necessarily as old as some of the earlier stories that are found in the beginning of the book. In fact, the simple fact that these tales involve King Arthur, a fifth- or sixth- century Romano-Celtic warrior chieftain, negates the idea that this text is pre-Christian. It is therefore much less likely that Chrétien simply took this preexisting text and altered it to suit his court's favor. It is much more likely that both works came from an earlier common source text such as the *Peveril*. Why then would a Christian artifact be so closely related to a Romano-Celtic chieftain, and in a way so similar to Celtic tales of magical cauldrons of the Underworld?

To fully examine such a perplexing subject, it is necessary to be well acquainted with the varying forms of this slippery, shifting object of veneration and ancient lore. While the Grail is traditionally held to be the cup or chalice used by Christ during the Last Supper, and the container used to collect remnants of His blood at the crucifixion, there are several other objects claimed to be the Grail. In all the texts dealing with the Grail, it has taken the form of a cup, a dish or bowl, a book, the Philosopher's Stone (an alchemical "crucible" of sorts), an emerald fallen from the crown of Lucifer as he fell from Heaven, the Shroud of Turin or burial shroud of Christ, the Ark of the Covenant, the womb of the Virgin Mary, and in more recent treatises, a lost bloodline or "line of descent" from a union between Jesus and Mary Magdalene.

Moving from the first accepted text forward, Chrétien failed to mention what the Grail was, or what form it took. When the description is given of what Perceval sees while seated with the Rich Fisher King, the procession is said to begin not with the Grail itself, but with a bleeding lance, apparently representative of the spear of Longinus which pierced the side of Christ. The Grail then appears being held between the hands of a maiden. The word Chrétien uses to name it is "graal," which some have interpreted as a type of serving dish or bowl. He goes on to describe it later as being made of refined gold, and set with precious stones.

After Perceval leaves the castle of the Rich Fisher King, he is chastised by a hermit in the woods, and is asked why he did not ask the all-important question. In this dialog, the statement is made, "...But do not think that he [The Fisher King] takes from it a pike, a lamprey, or a salmon. The holy man sustains and refreshes his life with a single mass wafer." Here the Grail does appear to be a dish or bowl large enough to hold a fish. It would have been truly fortunate if Chrétien had been able to complete his famous work, for then we could have an idea what was first meant by the word "graal." However, it was left to his continuators to complete the body of the Grail's legend.

Proceeding to the First Continuation, the Grail is again described as something in which food is served, but this time it requires no assistance to perform its service other than its own magical power. The Grail, now seen by Gawain instead of Perceval, floats around the hall filling the plates of the attendant knights with bread and their cups with wine, reminiscent of Christ's statement of bread being His body and the wine His blood. This similarity is soon questioned, however, as the Grail again passes each knight giving him the full portion of his favorite food as his need requires, as did the Celtic cauldron of plenty. Despite this reference to a Celtic symbol, the full history of the Grail is given in detail, including a peculiar twist.

It is true that Joseph caused it to be made: that Joseph of Arimathea who so loved the Lord all his life, as it seemed, that on the
day when he received the death on the cross to save sinners, Joseph
came with the Grail which he had caused to be made to Mount
Calvary, where God was crucified ... He placed it at once below
his feet, which were wet with blood which flowed down each foot,
and collected as much as he was able in this Grail of fine gold.

Here, the familiar tale of the Holy Grail catching the blood of
Christ at the crucifixion is first seen, as well as the role of Joseph of
Arimathea. The interesting part of this revelation is in the phrase, "...It
is true that Joseph caused it to be made." Traditionally, the Grail was
the cup used by Christ at the Last Supper, which would mean that the
cup would have already existed, presumably obtained by whomever held
the Last Supper, not made by Joseph on the occasion of Christ's
crucifixion. This calls into question the concept of the Grail as the cup
of the Last Supper. However, in future discussion of a vessel called the
"Santo Cáliz," there is an object that might fit the description of such
a cup made for Joseph.

To further confuse the issue, this text goes on to describe another
object described as a Grail. The story relates how Nicodemus, a secret
follower of Jesus, carved a head in the likeness of Christ, said to be closest to His true appearance. The Continuation further states that this
"Grail" carving may be seen in the town of Lucca, Italy. Surprisingly,
there is actually a carving of Christ, although in full body instead of
just the head, which can indeed be found in Lucca.

The next source book for the modern Grail hunter is Robert de
Boron's *Joseph d'Arimathie*. In it he records how, unlike Chrétien and
his continuators, he used an entirely different original book in which a
great deal of Christian history and secrets were inscribed. Here he relates
the story of Joseph and Nicodemus together requesting Christ's body
from Pilate, and how after His tomb is found empty, Joseph is imprisoned. There Joseph is given the holy relic by the resurrected Christ
himself, and instructed on the mysteries and rituals of the Holy Mass.
He remains in jail until AD 70, when he is freed by the Romans. After
his liberation, he takes his daughter and son-in-law, Bron, to the island
of Britain where he begins the family of Grail guardians that included
Joseph, Bron, Alein, and his son Perceval.

It is pointed out here that there is a great deal of time left out of
the equation. If Joseph is imprisoned until the year AD 70, how is
it possible that Perceval, contemporaneous with Arthur in the fifth

century, could have inherited the Grail in only three generations? This dilemma is quite magically solved in the *Didot Perceval*, in which Bron lives far beyond his normal life span due to the Grail's healing powers. Again, the anonymous author claims his source is purer than that of either Chrétien or de Boron, stating that he wrote from an original text written by someone named Blayse. This story relates how the Round Table is only the last of three tables surrounding the Grail—the first being that at which Christ sat at the Last Supper, the second table that of Joseph of Arimathea at which the first Eucharist was held, and last, the Round Table of Arthur which now served to bring the Grail back into the world and hearts of all good and holy men. It is also said that Bron, now hundreds of years old, is sick and can only be returned to health by the perfect knight who must come to him and ask the question, "What is it that the Grail has served and what is it that it serves?" When Perceval endeavors to find the Grail and enters the castle of the Rich Fisher King, he witnesses a procession much like that described by Chrétien. Perceval fails to ask the question and embarks on the journey to prove himself worthy of the Grail. He finally achieves the Grail and is told "the secret words which Joseph taught," much like the secrets of the Grail taught to Joseph by Jesus while imprisoned.

Wolfram von Eschenbach's *Parzifal* is the first diversion from the concept of the Grail being a relic of Christ's passion. Eschenbach claims that the Grail is actually a powerful stone, called the "Lapis Excillis," with which God cast Lucifer out of Heaven. Other than the fact that the Grail is now a damning stone instead of Christ's chalice, the story almost mirrors Chrétien's *The Story of the Grail*. This is not really surprising, as Wolfram claims that he used the same source book as Chrétien, except Wolfram claims the French cleric didn't do the original work justice. Wolfram claims to have obtained the original work from a mysterious figure named Kyot in Toledo, Spain, the original text having been an Arabic manuscript adapted by Chrétien to suit his European court.

One possible explanation of the Kyot reference could be Guiot de Provence, a supporter of and initiate in the order of the Knights Templar. Although debate rages over whether or not de Provence is Wolfram's Kyot, there appears to be substantial evidence to support this conclusion. However, the existence of Wolfram's contact, or of Kyot being Guiot de Provence, is inconsequential in the context of the story. The most important part of *Parzifal* is in the switch in the guardianship of the Grail. Wolfram changes the guardians of this sacred relic from the family of the Rich Fisher King to the Knights Templar, a theme that appears to have continued in *Perlesvaus*. Although the knights of the Grail feast are not named as Templars, their description seems to imply this association very clearly.

Now to the work that brought the Grail story into popular readership. The *Vulgate Cycle* contained two books, the first of which dealt with the failure of Arthur's knights to find the Holy Grail, and the second that dealt with Perceval and his attainment of the Grail. Of interest in this text is another suggestion that there are two Grails. The first Grail mentioned takes the form of a tiny but very important book, written by Jesus himself, which only the most holy could read. Upon reading this book, Arthur discovers the inscription, "This is the book of thy descent. Here begins the book of the Holy Grail." However, later in the text, the traditional Grail chalice is seen as well, described as being made not of wood, stone, metal, horn, or bone. In other words, it is distinguished as an object not of the material world.

This concept of two Grails is quite interesting, if not popular. Precisely what can be surmised about the Grail with so many different descriptions and characteristics? Once again, it is important to return to the source of the mystery. However, this time, the investigation will not stop at Chrétien's version of the Grail story. The next chapter returns to the very beginning of the Grail story. To learn its true nature, it is necessary to journey back to the very time of Christ, and learn what to expect at a holy tomb and a very important Passover meal.

3

THE LIFE AND DEATH OF CHRIST

Since the legend of the Grail is almost two thousand years old, it isn't surprising that there are so many differing accounts of it. It can be conceptualized in terms of a personal secret. For example, if a man has a hidden treasure, he might make an outward reference to it, or he might not. If he does leave some literary, textual mark pointing to its location, and if he values his treasure, he will make it as difficult to decipher as possible. This means that he will create a riddle which very few, or possibly only he, will be able to understand. Therefore, if this man dies without passing the knowledge on to someone else, the secret becomes lost or nearly impossible to discover.

Now, after hundreds of years have passed, and assuming the man has indeed left a trace of his wealth behind, someone else stumbles across his riddle. This person takes his or her own biases, affiliations, and cultural colorations into account when the riddle is read. If this individual then wishes to make further reference to the hidden gold, that person's words are added to the existing evidence left behind by the first person.

Then the second person dies without finding the treasure. The next person, or next ten people to undertake the investigation add their own pieces to the *legend* of the great hidden treasure. By now, several hundred years later, the original information is so muted and disguised by later works, it has become more widely known, but more difficult to correctly understand.

31

It's something like a thousand-year-old game of "telephone." Each person understands differently than the last, and depending on the character or intentions of each individual, the story becomes adjusted accordingly. Each fact is given the outward bias of the popular view of the time. In fact, this becomes a concern while investigating Chrétien's Grail account. Is the whole story simply another fictional tale created for courtly amusement, or did it begin with some simple historical truth?

The true task at hand for anyone researching a historical mystery is to look at the "big picture." Returning to the previous treasure analogy, if the job of finding the lost gold is to be undertaken, it is necessary to look not only at the hint given by the first person, or the multiple opinions left behind by the next seven or eight researchers, but also at other unintentional clues. One must look at the geographical location of the first man, his beliefs, his character, what he thought was important, and finally, how his contemporaries reacted toward him.

These hints can be put together with the original tale, and with what seem to be recurring themes throughout other relevant texts, to create a framework over which can be reassembled the events that form the reality of the original event—the simple hiding of a treasure chest, or in the case of the Grail, the simple use of a cup.

After gaining familiarity with the concept of looking at the root of a matter, look at the absolute beginning of the Grail legend—the Last Supper and crucifixion. To understand the nature of the Grail, there must be an understanding of what these two originating events were and what someone living at the time might expect to see at both.

The Last Supper was held as a Passover seder—the ritual meal commemorating the ancient Jewish tradition of Moses. During the time of the Hebrew enslavement in Egypt, Moses requested freedom for his people from Pharaoh. When Pharaoh refused, and mocked the god of Moses, Moses told Pharaoh that there would be numerous plagues sent down to his land by God, among which was the death of the first-born son. To prevent this curse from happening to his own people, Moses instructed them to mark their doors with the blood of a young goat or lamb, which they were to prepare as a feast. Afterward, they must close themselves in their homes to avoid the coming angel of death, sent by God to claim the first-born son of all the land, including that of the king of Egypt. Following the death of his first-born son, Pharaoh freed Moses and all of the enslaved Hebrews.

Although the Passover was a Jewish custom, Christ used this to begin a practice that would later become one of the most important rituals of Christianity. Anticipating His own impending capture and death, Christ instructed His disciples to take the bread He gave them and eat it, as it was His body which He gave them. Then, He gave them wine that He said was the blood of His covenant with mankind. Christ said that this practice was to be performed in remembrance of Him, because He was soon to leave them. At this time, the others with Him asked where He was going, and why. He then related to them what was to come, and that one of their own would betray Him into the hands of the Romans. It was soon revealed that Judas would be the one to put the events in motion which would lead to Christ's crucifixion. A short time after that, Jesus was arrested in the Garden of Gethsemane, tried, convicted, and crucified on the hill of Golgotha.

What does the Bible say about specific aspects of these places, such as their location and the nature of the settings? The only geographical location mentioned is Golgotha, a place meaning "The Place of the Skull," which has been located with some certainty. However, little is actually said about the location of the Last Supper other than that it was held in an "upper room." Unfortunately, this tells little of the actual location. The standard configuration of a Jewish home of the time was to have a business or shop on the ground floor of the dwelling with living quarters on the second floor (or upper room), the cooking to be done on the roof to take advantage of natural ventilation. Although this alone doesn't tell much, other aspects of the whole story may shed light on the location and nature of the Last Supper.

Earlier in the story, Jesus and his followers searched for a place to hold this Passover meal. Instructions were given to go to the town well and wait for a man with a pitcher of water. As instructed, two of His followers went to the well and waited. Finally, the man with his pitcher came and the disciples followed him to the house where he entered, asking the master of the house to use the second story guest chamber for the Passover meal. There is much speculation about who this person was and who hosted this famous meal. In the city of Jerusalem, there is a site called the "Cenacle" where tourists come to see what is called the place of the Last Supper.

Although the exact physical location is not important, it is important to learn more about the exact nature or "style" of the Last Supper. Was it a rich and sumptuous feast, or was it a simple, poor meal with simple trappings? Throughout the Bible, Jesus is seen to be a simple man, appreciative of simple ways. Therefore, the meal may have been as simple as any average person's table—simple food, with basic wooden or clay plates and bowls. It is debated whether there would have been separate drinking vessels or if they simply drank from small bowls. Most likely this would have depended upon the wealth of the house in question.

Although it seems that Christ would have favored a house of simplicity, this is not necessarily the case. We must remember that Christ himself did not choose the location. It was chosen by chance or God's will. In this case, the individual in question may have come from the house of a slightly more wealthy family, who would have had items of higher quality than average. Although there are many possibilities, there are a few different theories considered to be the most likely scenarios. The following is found in the *Catholic Encyclopedia*'s entry for "Last Supper."

> The owner of the house in which was the upper room of the Last Supper is not mentioned in Scripture; but he must have been one of the disciples, since Christ bids Peter and John say, "The Master says." Some say it was Nicodemus, or Joseph of Arimathea, or the mother of John Mark. The hall was large and furnished as a dining-room. In it Christ showed Himself after His Resurrection; here took place the election of Matthias to the Apostolate and the sending of the Holy Ghost; here the first Christians assembled for the breaking of bread; hither Peter and John came when they had given testimony after the cure of the man born lame, and Peter after his liberation from prison; here perhaps was the council of the Apostles held. It was for awhile the only church in Jerusalem, the mother of all churches, known as the Church of the Apostles or of Sion. It was visited in 404 by St. Paula of Rome. In the eleventh century it was destroyed by the Saracens, later rebuilt and given to the care of the Augustinians. Restored after a second destruction, it was placed in charge of the Franciscans, who were driven out in 1561. At present it is a Moslem mosque.

The above passage states that some possibilities for the Last Supper's location were the homes of "Nicodemus, or Joseph of Arimathea, or the mother of John Mark." Since at least two of these were considered as their society's upper class, this would increase the range of potential dinnerware from clay or wooden items to those made of Roman glass. Archeological digs such as those in Caesarea have uncovered a great deal of simple, mass-produced Roman glassware available in this time. It could have been that such people were able to obtain items of this quality.

The possibility that the Last Supper was held in the house of Joseph of Arimathea adds another interesting consideration to the question. Although not one of Christ's disciples, Joseph was a secret follower as stated in the gospels, requesting the body of Christ from Pilate after the crucifixion. If this were the case, the potential richness of the meal may have been much greater than originally imagined. Joseph of Arimathea was a merchant of metals throughout what is now Europe, as well as a member of the Jewish supreme council or Sanhedrin. It is clear that Joseph was a very wealthy man in his time, and that if he were the host of the Last Supper, the material of which a historical Grail may have been made could be almost anything available at the time. Although this Grail may have been made from metal, even gold or silver, this would have been very unlikely. Although Joseph was a wealthy man, possessions made of gold were usually found only in the dwelling of royalty. It is obvious that he was not of this class since he was to be buried in a stone tomb instead of a marvelous crypt, as would be a member of royalty.

In both of these situations, the possibility of potentially opulent settings for the Last Supper exists, but the most likely scenario would have been relatively simple. According to authorities on ancient Hebraic traditions, the type of plates and bowls used probably would have been clay or ceramic, simple in form and function, and if any separate drinking vessels were used, they too would have been plain. However, there is the possibility of wood or even glass objects being present. If the owner of the house was a follower of Christ, it is conceivable that finer items might have been used since such a celebrated man would hold a holy day observance there. Although these materials were not commonly found on ancient Jewish tables, such items might have been considered the ancient day equivalent of the "good china."

With regard to the Grail, the real conundrum begins with the crucifixion. Why was this cup present at both a religious meal and in Christ's tomb? Was this typical of the time, or was it completely contrary to accepted practice? Before these questions can be answered, the specific characteristics of the crucifixion must be investigated.

Even in the time of the Roman Empire, crucifixion was a particularly severe punishment reserved for the most grievous crimes. The practice was to drive spikes through both feet, and through the small open area in the bones of each wrist, into the heavy wood of the cross. Crucifixion crosses took a few different forms. The most well known today is that of the cross bar striking the upright beam roughly four-fifths of the distance from the ground. Other forms are T-shaped, X-shaped, or even some that are simply one upright beam.

The purpose of death by crucifixion was not to allow the accused to bleed to death from the grievous wounds inflicted by the nails. The postmortem of a crucified individual would have almost certainly determined death by asphyxiation. In hanging a person on a crucifix, the pain of the nails driven through one's extremities would have been secondary to the crushing weight of the victim's own body, making it almost impossible to breathe. When a person's body hangs from their hands or arms, it creates a constriction that does not allow the lungs to intake a full amount of air. Therefore, death was caused most often by either suffocation or by the strain placed on the heart. The accused usually died fairly quickly after being lifted into place. However, if the victim lingered, the practice was to break his legs to speed the process of asphyxiation.

It was a custom at this time of the year for the Roman Magistrate to free one prisoner sentenced to death to foster amity between the Jews and their rulers. Therefore, when Pilate asked the people whom he should release, Jesus or Barabbas the thief, the crowd cheered for the release of Barabbas. His conscience cleared, Pilate stated that Jesus should be forced to drag His heavy cross through the streets of Jerusalem until He reached the site of His death. His clothes torn from His body and replaced by a crown of thorns, He was to be nailed to the crosspiece and raised over the jubilant audience to die.

The dilemma at Christ's crucifixion was that the Sabbath was rapidly approaching, and it was considered ritualistically unclean to handle a dead body on the Sabbath. Therefore, in the attempt to complete the crucifixion before the holy day arrived, the Roman soldiers standing ready planned to break His legs, assuming this would bring His death. However the centurion Longinus determined it would be better to pierce His heart. As a result, he stabbed his spear into Christ's side, and determined He was already dead. According to legend, this act completed the prophecy that the Messiah would be known because His death would come without one bone of His body being broken. The legend continues that a small portion of Christ's blood fell upon the eyes of the blind centurion, and instantly he was able to see. As we will see later, Longinus plays an important part in the Grail legend and that of the Spear of Destiny, as it would come to be known.

After Jesus's body was taken down from the cross by Joseph of Arimathea, and in some accounts by Nicodemus as well, His body was lain in a new tomb intended for Joseph himself. Once there, His body was wrapped in Joseph's fine shroud, thus beginning another legend—the Shroud of Turin. Before the tomb was sealed, Nicodemus brought rich oils and balms with which to anoint Jesus's body. According to the Grail legend, it was either here or at the foot of the cross, while Christ's body was being lowered, that Joseph collected the shed blood before the body was wrapped in the shroud.

Ancient Hebrew funerary practices must now be taken into account to determine if the cup of the Last Supper truly found its way into the tomb or why it is mentioned in this context. The customary practice when someone died was to take the body to the family's home and anoint it with oils and herbs, not as a preservative as did the Egyptians, but as a final tribute to honor the deceased loved one. Since references state that this practice was done in an upper room, this might have been how the cup of the Last Supper found its way to the preparation of Christ's body. If His body was taken to the same location as the Passover meal, the cup could have been used as a type of communal container, holding whatever was necessary instead of just wine. This hypothesis became especially appealing because of the reference to Joseph of Arimathea being Christ's uncle—a reference that will be revisited in the next chapter.

However, this point soon becomes moot upon rereading the four Gospels. Each says the same thing in relation to the time between Christ's body being taken down from the cross to the time the tomb is found empty. As stated above, His body was removed from the cross due to the rapidly impending holy day of Sabbath, then taken to the new tomb of Joseph, where it was anointed with oils and herbs and then wrapped in the shroud. The account of Mary Magdalene's bringing oils for Christ's body happened only after the tomb was found empty. However, in the book of Matthew, chapter 27, verses 55 through 61, the manner in which Mary Magdalene was present at the crucifixion and the entombment is described.

> There were also many women there, looking on from afar, who had followed Jesus from Galilee, ministering to him; among whom were Mary Magdalene, and Mary the mother of James and Joseph, and the mother of the sons of Zebedee.
> When it was evening, there came a rich man from Arimathea, named Joseph, who also was a disciple of Jesus. He went to Pilate and asked for the body of Jesus. Then Pilate ordered it to be given to him. And Joseph took the body, and wrapped it in a clean linen

shroud, and laid it in his own new tomb, which he had hewn in
the rock; and he rolled a great stone to the door of the tomb, and
departed. Mary Magdalene and the other Mary were there, sitting
opposite the sepulchre.

There are two times between the crucifixion and entombment at
which blood could have been collected—just after the body was taken
down from the cross, and while preparing Christ's body inside the tomb.

It was the custom of Jewish burial that all spilled blood was collected in a container and entombed with the body. This included any
blood spilled on the ground at the foot of the cross or any objects that
might have blood still on them, like the spear of Longinus, or the Roman
flagrums that were used to whip Jesus before crucifixion. Therefore, the
blood that fell on the ground at the foot of the cross must have been
collected just after Christ's body was taken down. This blood and dirt
was then placed in a container to be entombed with the body, along with
the other items listed above.

Blood was probably also collected during the hasty preparation of
Christ's body. In many depictions of a corpse being prepared for burial, there is a scene in which the blood from a wound drains into a shallow cup. Considering the short time between the removal of the body
and its placement in the tomb, it can rightly be assumed that blood was
still issuing from the body. The Gospel of John states that Pilate is sur-
prised that Jesus had already died, and that He had not been dead long
when Joseph requested His body.

This theory is supported by another source of legendary origin. The
stains of liquid blood can be seen on the Shroud of Turin image.
Although this debated relic is not proof, it does demonstrate that it was
widely accepted that liquid blood still flowed from Christ's body as it
was prepared for burial. There is also an image from Glastonbury of
Joseph of Arimathea that depicts him holding the Holy Grail, not in
the form of a chalice, but in the form of two vials or flasks.

To review: The Holy Grail as the cup of the Last Supper might
have become the cup that held Christ's blood after the normal post-
crucifixion ritual of preparing the body in an upper room of a relative's
dwelling had taken place. However, normal practices could not have
been performed in their entirety due to the rapidly approaching holy
day. They did perform the Hebrew funerary practice of blood collection in two ways—scooping up the dirt from the foot of the cross (and
any blood that spilled on the ground from Golgotha to the tomb), and
again while preparing the body inside the tomb.

This presents an interesting dilemma. Instead of having the single cup of the Grail legend, the cup of the Last Supper and the vessel used to collect the blood relics after the crucifixion, there exists the dual aspect of two vessels being used to collect the blood. Which of these vessels is the real Grail, if one ever existed? Since the containers in question were handled by those who prepared Christ's body for entombment, those characters should be examined to see if they can shed some light on this curious aspect of the Grail legend.

4

GUARDIANS OF
THE BLOOD

The problem in making connections in a historical mystery is not in finding the clues. History is nothing but clues, to any number of things, which may or may not seem to be related to your needs. The challenge one faces is in taking the factual clues one finds throughout history, and deducing which question these would best answer. Oddly enough, other questions which do not seem to fit in anywhere often provide the connection. They provide a certain context, without which only a best guess can be used to solve the mystery. One must remember that it requires three points to assign a location to an object in three-dimensional space. It likewise often requires several questions and only one answer to pinpoint a historical fact.

While legend indicates that Joseph was the most likely candidate for the collector of Christ's blood, there were two other Biblical characters present who in some way participated in the funerary practices. Also, there is the question of how the Grail could have been both the cup of the Last Supper and the holder of His blood inside the tomb which requires an answer. While the latter topic is to be the conclusion of this book, the persons of Joseph of Arimathea, Nicodemus, and Mary Magdalene can be dealt with presently.

In almost every Grail text, Joseph of Arimathea is cited as the one person who begins the Grail legend by collecting Christ's blood in it at the crucifixion. One might wonder why it was Joseph and not one of the disciples of Jesus who collected the blood, took the body from the cross, and gave his own new tomb for Christ's burial.

The answer can be found in an old legend which is well known around the Southern part of England. This tradition states that Joseph of Arimathea was related to Jesus, and might actually have been His great-uncle, that is to say, the younger brother of the father of Mary. Although this legend may at first seem a little far-fetched, let us consider a few relevant points. The body of a crucified man would have become the property and concern of a family member after death under both Hebrew and Roman law. This and the fact that the disciples were somewhat seen as criminals might explain why one of them did not take such a role in Christ's burial. Therefore, Joseph would have been the next male in Jesus's immediate family whose responsibility it was to take care of the burial preparations.

The legend of Joseph further states that he took the young Jesus and His mother to England during the "twelve lost years" of Jesus's life which are not accounted for in Biblical accounts. It is said that after the death of Joseph, Jesus's father, Joseph of Arimathea took the remainder of His family to the British Isles where he often went as a metal merchant, most likely trading in tin from the Mindip Hills. This tradition is reflected in many depictions of Joseph standing in a boat accompanied by the boy Jesus. The idea of Joseph being part of the "Holy Family" adds an interesting aspect to the Grail legend. This is the most likely reason why Joseph would have gone to Britain with a small party of early Christians after the death of Christ—he had lived there with Jesus in previous years. What better place to commemorate His life and continue in His teachings than in that place where both had once lived?

Here we begin learning about what are called the Traditions of Glastonbury, involving Joseph, the Grail, and what the early church vehemently maintained was the first Christian church in Europe. As we have read, Joseph brought some of Christ's followers here after the crucifixion. As legend would have it, this group journeyed through the Mediterranean, around the Iberian Penninsula, and eventually found their way to the coast of Britain where they sailed down a river leading inland to the place we now call Glastonbury. This band of travellers then ascended a hill to look over the land that would one day house the great Glastonbury Abbey. On soil that was strange to them, weary from their travels, the early missionaries proclaimed this their new home atop what is now appropriately called "Wearyall Hill"—the place where a

Thorn Tree grows on the spot that Joseph reputedly struck with his staff into the wet ground.

Around AD 63, the group built the first church out of wattle (a type of mud, branch, and grass construction) on the site of the dwelling in which Joseph, Jesus, and Mary had once lived. This site is now covered by the ruins of the Lady Chapel and was consecrated as the site of the old church in 1186.

This church was accepted as late as the fifteenth century by several church councils, stating that none of the churches of France or Spain were the first Christian churches in Europe. Rather it was Glastonbury which could claim that right. The Domesday Book even records that King Avaragus granted the famous twelve hides of land to this church—land which had never before paid tax.

We see here that the church at Glastonbury was indeed ancient in origin, dating from the first century. But what can we tell about Joseph's part in the Grail legend with respect to Glastonbury? Varying legends speak of Joseph burying the Grail at the foot of Glastonbury Tor, a great tower-surmounted hill near the Abbey, in an underground stream which even today flows from a fountain looking and tasting like blood. However, this legend appears to be created later in history.

What we do know of the early legends of Joseph coming to Glastonbury is that he indeed came with the holy relics of Christ's blood, only with these not in a chalice, but in two cruets—two small containers filled with Jesus's blood and sweat. While these are certainly different than the Grail we have read about Joseph having upon his arrival to Britain, the account is just the same. Only the form of the relic varies. Was this simply a mistake made over countless years, making two Grails into one? How has the cup of the Last Supper become two small containers?

To further confuse issues, one of our originating texts describes how there is a Grail of another form, this time associated with Nicodemus, which is nowhere near Glastonbury or Joseph and his early church. This somewhat separate legend is set forth in what is called the First Continuation, written in 1190 in the attempt to finish Chrétien's incomplete Grail romance.

> Nicodemus had carved and fashioned a head in the likeness of the Lord on the day that he had seen Him on the cross. But of this I am sure, that the Lord God set His hand to the shaping of it, as they say; for no man ever saw one like it nor could it be made by

human hands. Most of you who have been at Lucca know it and have seen this Grail... [Capt, *The Traditions of Glastonbury*].

Although this text states that Joseph of Arimathea left this "Grail" at Lucca on the way to Britain, history tells a different story about the origin of the carving in Lucca. Although it consists of a full-body crucifix instead of just a head, the Volto Santo is said to have been carved by Nicodemus. After his death, the Volto Santo was passed from Nicodemus to Isaachar (Isaac), in whose home the relic was secretly worshipped for many years.

Then in 742 during the Iconoclastic Period, Selenco, the guardian of the relic at this time, removed it to Lucca, Italy, for safekeeping. Some time after the bishop Walfried of Italy received the carving, he found two vials of blood in the neck of the statue near the base of the skull, carefully hidden away. This carving can still be seen there today in the Chapel of San Martino, and the blood relic can be seen in the Chapel of the Holy Blood in San Frediano.

Here we see another instance of two vials of blood being found in a relic referred to as the Grail, in relation to yet another obscure follower of Jesus. This makes matters very interesting indeed. Joseph was said to have arrived at Britain with two small containers of Christ's blood, to which the Grail legend is attributed. Now we have Nicodemus, the man who came to Jesus in the Garden of Gethsemane and asked how a man who is already born could be born again, who is also apparently in possession of two vials containing blood relics.

Although it is possible that Nicodemus obtained these blood relics while assisting Joseph in the preparation of Christ's body, as described in the Gospel of John, chapter 19, verse 39, how does Nicodemus fit into the traditional Grail legend originating with Joseph of Arimathea? Further, how does one resolve all these possible Grails—the container holding the bloody dirt from the foot of the cross, the cup into which drained the blood from a wound in Christ's body, Olympiodorus's Marian Chalice, the cup of the Last Supper, and now four cruets which belonged to Joseph and Nicodemus?

To answer these questions, one must consult the best historical resource we have pertaining to the Grail. As Graham Phillips states utilizing the account given by Olympiodorus in the fifth century, one possible historical Grail is referred to as the Marian Chalice. Since this is the earliest living mention of the Grail, long before Chrétien wrote his "The Story of the Grail," one must give it credence. However, this reference associates Mary Magdalene, not Joseph, with the Holy Grail. What reason could there be for this variant version of the Grail's genesis? Returning to the Phillips book, one possible explanation is given.

> If the Marian Chalice did inspire the theme of the Holy Grail as the cup of Christ, then the story of Joseph bringing the Grail to Britain would be inaccurate. The Marian Chalice was only discovered in AD 327 by the Empress Helena in the Holy Sepulchre in Jerusalem. Neither was it associated with Joseph of Arimathea, but with Mary Magdalene. There may, however, have been a confusion of two separate traditions.
>
> ...St. John's Gospel relates how Mary Magdalene had visited the Holy Sepulchre to find the tomb empty and a late Grail romance written around 1225 by the French poet Gerbert de Montreuil (sometimes called the Fourth Continuation) says that Joseph had obtained the Grail from Mary on the day of the Resurrection. Perhaps such a legend already existed during the Empress Helena's time, a legend coupling the Grail with both Mary Magdalene and Joseph of Arimathea.
>
> ...The Gerbert romance suggests that a legend could have survived that Joseph had obtained the cup from Mary. Perhaps it was thought that the cup remained in, or was later returned to the tomb by Joseph himself. Such a legend may have led Empress Helena to believe that the cup she found in the Holy Sepulchre had been used by Mary Magdalene to collect Christ's blood, while at the same time believing it to be the same vessel used at the Last Supper.

Here we see an array of apparent discrepancies in the Grail story. First, was it Joseph or Mary who first obtained the Grail? Was it sent to Britain with Joseph or by the Roman Emperor Honorius nearly three centuries later? Finally, was this paradox the result of two separate occurrences that were erroneously merged into one legend—the cup of the Last Supper and a vessel containing Christ's shed blood?

There is one thing of which one can be sure. Olympiodorus mentions a cup called the Marian Chalice which was sent to Britain in AD 410 to protect it during the attacks on Rome. This places it as a real object in a time much earlier than when the Grail romances were written. Looking at the author of this account, Olympiodorus can be trusted as a reliable, objective historical source because he was not himself a Christian, and he did not attempt to promote a Christian agenda. Further, Olympiodorus has been used as a credible historical reference by many modern historians. Therefore, we see that he provides us with the most historically stable reference marker in researching the existence of the Grail. However, this doesn't resolve our Mary Magdalene problem. Did the Grail come from Mary Magdalene or from Joseph?

A study of the person who was Mary is a truly interesting study. She is seen varyingly as a prostitute, a secret disciple, a companion, possibly the wife of Jesus, and finally as a combination of many different female characters of the Bible. While the recent theories describing Mary Magdalene as the secret lover, wife, and mother of Christ's children adds a new dimension to the Grail legend, close examination reveals that the theory is too dependent on the claims of a power-hungry empire, seeking to ground its claim to leadership in a holy, royal bloodline. A historical study of Mary is difficult at best, but from what we have in the Grail legend, and from other legends regarding Mary Magdalene, we can infer a few things.

Although Mary's specific characteristics cannot be proven, many Biblical scholars see Mary as a follower of Jesus, and she may well have been as close to Jesus as was Nicodemus. This theory is justified by recalling the Bible story of Mary anointing the body of Jesus before the Last Supper from John 12:1–7.

> Six days before the Passover, Jesus arrived at Bethany, where Lazarus lived, whom Jesus had raised from the dead. Here a dinner was given in Jesus' honor. Martha served, while Lazarus was among those reclining at the table with him. Then Mary took about a pint of pure nard, an expensive perfume; she poured it on Jesus' feet and wiped his feet with her hair. And the house was filled with the fragrance of the perfume. But one of his disciples, Judas Iscariot, who was later to betray him, objected, "Why wasn't this perfume sold and the money given to the poor? It was worth a year's wages." He did not say this because he cared about the poor but because he was a thief; as keeper of the money bag, he used to help himself to what was put into it. "Leave her alone," Jesus replied. "[It was intended] that she should save this perfume for the day of my burial."

By Mary Magdalene using oils to anoint Jesus's body, she performed a ritual referred to as preparations for Christ's burial. Therefore we can assume that the container in which this oil is held now has the signifigance of a funerary object, which would have given it an almost sacred importance of its own.

This may also shed light on our delemma of resolving the Grail as an object used in death as well as an object related to the Last Supper. In this story, we see Jesus at a feast given in His honor, with Mary Magdalene in attendance along with Martha, her sister. We can justly assume that these are followers of Christ. Although most accounts state that it was only Jesus and His disciples at the Last Supper, some others say that there may have been many there in attendance, including women. Surely, if this were the case, Mary Magdalene would have been one of these female followers. After these events, she would have cherished the object that held the oils, as it now linked her in a special way to the importance of Jesus's life and death.

The only other mention of Mary throughout history is a legend regarding her last 30 years, spent in a life of penance in a cave at Sainte Baume in France. It states that she, her sister Martha, her brother Lazarus, and St. Maximin came to the forests of the Ligurians, bringing with them a vial of Christ's blood. This blood relic is now allegedly kept in Sainte Maximin where it was displayed as recently as 1876.

Now there is Mary Magdalene, yet another person possessing a vial of Christ's blood. Is this the Marian Chalice found by Empress Helena in the tomb? How could it be, if it were sent to Britain in AD 410? Besides, what about that vessel in which she kept the oils used to anoint Christ's feet a week before the Last Supper?

So far, there have been four different stories, all of which have historical backing, each one referring to objects which may be called the Holy Grail. The classical version of the Grail legend states that the Grail was the cup of the Last Supper in which Joseph caught Christ's blood during His crucifixion. However, we have seen that two objects would have been used to catch Christ's blood—one to scoop up the blood-stained dirt, and one into which the blood from a wound, say the spear wound in Christ's side, would have drained. Besides these discrepancies, there are also the questions of Joseph's two vials of Christ's blood, the two belonging to Nicodemus which were found inside the Volto Santo, and at least one belonging to Mary Magdalene when she and her family found their way to Southern France.

To understand the way in which these separate traditions come together, it is necessary to delve into the annals of history. The Grail has featured in several important points in the history of the western world stretching from the time of Christ, through the Crusades, into modern times. Therefore, further investigation of the Grail legend must begin at the place where the legend itself began—the Isle of Glass, the place where Joseph brought his Holy Grail.

5

GLASTONBURY, GATEWAY TO AVALON

The medieval legends of King Arthur and the Grail, however else they may be linked, are no more closely associated than in the mystical realm of Avalon. It is there where Arthur is taken on the magical barge after his fateful battle at Camlaan. It is there, at the place called "the Isle of Glass," where the Grail hero finds himself in his pursuit of the holy chalice. Where other than in the Arthurian and Grail texts can such an island be found? Is this a place of pure fantasy, or simply an image of the Celtic underworld? History and archeology can provide a glimpse of a different side of Avalon. The beginning of one's understanding of the true nature of a historical Grail must begin here. In the once marshy region of Somerset in southern England, history, archeology, and legend come together in one place. Variously called Ynys Witrin, Glass Island, and the Isle of Apples, today's Avalon is known by another name — Glastonbury.

Any investigation of Arthurian Britain or Grail-related sites will invariably end up at Glastonbury. On the grounds of the Abbey ruins, there is a large, wooden cross which best sums up the history of this site, its display stating that this holy place is so ancient that "only legend can record its origin." Legend relates how Joseph of Arimathea took the Grail, along with his small band of Christian pilgrims, from Palestine to Britain, settling in this area of Somerset where the ruins of Glastonbury Abbey now remain.

The importance of this event is quite easy to see around the area—in the windows of the churches, in the signs and plaques of the town's inns and pubs, and in the tourist centers and gift shops. As is the case with any other famous place, the legend has almost outgrown the truth of the site. However, if one is to understand Glastonbury's importance to the search for the true Grail, it is necessary to break down all the preconceived notions and opinions and try to discover the history of this truly mythical site.

The history one normally sees of Glastonbury Abbey is one much like many other abbeys throughout the Middle Ages—"fund raisers" touting relics of all kinds, ranging from fragments from the bones of saints to alleged relics from the Passion of Christ. This, combined with the claim that King Arthur's bones were discovered here, makes it quite easy to see why Glastonbury is thought of as a "factory of falsehoods." However, one has only to scratch this dirty surface to discover Glastonbury's deep and ancient history.

Augustine's visit to Glastonbury in AD 600 serves to cement the notion of the site's ancient, revered nature. The following is a section from a letter written by Augustine to Pope Gregory in Rome.

> In the Western confines of Britain—
> There is a certain Royal Island of large extent,
> Surrounded by water and abounding in all
> The beauties of Nature and necessities of life.
> In it, the first neophytes of Catholic Law
> Found a church constructed by no human art,
> But by the Hands of Christ Himself.
> [Capt, *The Traditions of Glastonbury*]

This reflects the idea, which was accepted up through the fifteenth century, that Glastonbury was the first Christian church in Europe, founded by Joseph of Arimathea in the first century AD (as discussed on page 42).

History states that Saint Patrick first brought Christianity to the British Isles around AD 433, meeting with some resistance initially. However, both local traditions and some historical records indicate that Saint Patrick was not the first to spread Christianity to this Celtic land. An early history of Glastonbury entitled *The Chronicle of Glastonbury Abbey* states that Patrick found a Christian community already flourishing in this area.

> Writing in the mid-fourteenth century, John of Glastonbury tells us that until the coming of St. Patrick in the fifth century there

was an unbroken succession of twelve hermits living at Glastonbury; they had no leader and were always twelve in number in
memory of the twelve companions who first settled the spot under
the leadership of St. Joseph of Arimathea [Carley, *Glastonbury
Abbey*, p. 2].

The history of Joseph traveling to Britain along with an unnum-
bered group of companions is first described in Robert de Boron's Joseph
d' Arimathie. This book describes how Joseph was imprisoned after the
body of Christ was found missing from the tomb in which He had been
placed. After being miraculously freed from his cell, Joseph takes the
cup of the Last Supper, the Grail, from which he had received suste-
nance during his captivity, and carries it to a distant land in the company of several other followers of Christ. It may at first seem odd that
Joseph and his fellow travelers would journey so far from their native
Palestine in search of a new place to live and spread the Gospel. However, another aspect of the Traditions of Glastonbury may shed some
light on this decision, reflecting a tradition of Joseph being in Britain
long before this famous journey.

John's Gospel in the Bible gives the reader a vivid picture of the
events surrounding the death of Christ. In approaching Pilate to ask
for Christ's body after crucifixion, Joseph risked his social standing,
and indeed his safety. Under both Roman and Hebrew laws, the only
legitimate individual who may make such a request of Pilate would be
the next immediate member of the family, preferably a male family
member such as a father, brother, or uncle. One may wonder why those
closest to Jesus, his disciples, did not ask for His body so that they could
make sure it was protected. Capt's *The Traditions of Glastonbury* again
makes a bold statement that Joseph of Arimathea was in fact related to
Jesus, most likely His great-uncle.

Legend states that Joseph was the younger brother of Mary's
father, thus making him Mary's uncle and Jesus's great-uncle. The connection between Glastonbury and Joseph's role in Jesus's early life has
to do with Joseph's trade. The Bible states that Joseph was a wealthy
man, able to afford a new rock-hewn tomb and all the finest trappings
to prepare for his burial, all of which were used for Christ's burial. This
would indicate that he was a merchant of some type.

Glastonbury tradition, as well as several historical sources, claim
that Joseph was a metal merchant, specifically dealing in the tin trade.
The tin used throughout the Roman Empire came mostly from the
areas around Pilton and the Mindip Hills. This theory is further

validated by the claims of many biblical scholars that the journey to Egypt, made by the Holy Family just after Christ's birth, would have been almost impossible unless they had some family relation there, or at least a member of the family who was more familiar with this foreign land. Surely Joseph would have had dealings with Egypt, perhaps to buy gold or other precious metals there. Indeed, one of the modern day candidates for the historical Grail is made from a red agate from Egypt.

Joseph's relationship with Jesus, although controversial, is a very important factor to consider when doing a historical analysis of the Glastonbury region. Almost everywhere around Glastonbury one can see images of Joseph in a sailing vessel with the young Christ at the head, images of a youthful Christ in both paintings and on the rare Tunic crosses, not to mention the myriad local stories corroborating the legend. Although this aspect of Glastonbury tradition seems a little farfetched at first, there are yet again certain undeniable facts which must be considered and which lend themselves to the theory.

Around the mining regions in this area, the ruined buildings that played a part in the mining trade are referred to as "Jew's Houses," illustrating the presence of Hebrew traders in metals in this region of Southern Britain. Similarly, the place names and folklore of the area further demonstrate the historicity of this theory. One of the ancient mines in this area is called "Corpus Christi," Latin for the "body of Christ." Similarly, the metal workers sing a peculiar chant while preparing their tin, stating, "Joseph was in the Tin Trade—the Tin Trade—the Tin Trade." The thought of Joseph and the boy Jesus visiting the green hills of Glastonbury is best witnessed in the hymn "Jerusalem" written by William Blake in response to this tradition.

> And did those feet in ancient time
> Walk upon England's mountains green?
> And was the Holy Lamb of God
> On England's pleasant pastures seen?
> And did the countenance divine
> Shine forth upon our clouded hills?
> And was Jerusalem builded here
> Among these dark satanic mills.
>
> Bring me my bow of burning gold!
> Bring me my arrows of desire!
> Bring me my spear! O Clouds unfold!
> Bring me my chariot of fire!

I will not cease from mental fight
Nor shall my sword sleep in my hand
Till we have built Jerusalem
In England's green and pleasant land.

Regardless of whether or not one believes that Joseph brought the boy Christ to Britain, there is little doubt that Joseph began a small Christian community at Glastonbury toward the end of the first century. Considering Saint Patrick's discovery of a preexisting Christian church upon his arrival in Britain, and the early mention of this church by Augustine in his letter to Pope Gregory, there can be little doubt that there was indeed an early Christian community there at Glastonbury. To better understand the nature of this community and their way of life, we must learn more about the story of their arrival and the nature of the land at this time.

As the legend goes, Joseph was imprisoned by the Romans after Christ's body was discovered missing from His tomb. After several years in confinement, fed only by a single mass wafer placed in the Grail by a dove descended from Heaven, Joseph is freed from his captivity. He then gathers a few people together, including his daughters and their husbands, one of which was named Bron, and travels with them to the distant land of Britain. Although very little is known about this journey, or for that matter the people who took it with Joseph, there are certain common threads that seem to form a quasi history around which we can make some inferences.

If one assumes Joseph traveled the same route he did while dealing in the metal trade, one can deduce from records of the Phoenician trade routes that the ship traveled through the Mediterranean Sea, probably making frequent stops along the way. An associated legend, that of Mary Magdalene and the Cult of the Black Virgin, would indicate that the southeastern coast of France was among these stops. Here in the areas around Sainte Baume and Sainte Maximin, the legend of Mary Magdalene settling in this region is quite well known. In fact, it was here that the uncorrupted body of Mary was allegedly found, along with a white alabaster jar containing some small amount of a blood relic.

From here, still following the old trade routes, the ship carrying Joseph and the remainder of his company would have sailed through the Straits of Gibraltar, out into the more dangerous waters of the ocean. Rounding the Spanish coast, these legendary wanderers would have nearly arrived at their final destination. Once they had reached the cool climes and green hills of Britain, they would have found a land very different from that of today's England.

When Joseph and his companions arrived at their new home, the ground on which Glastonbury Abbey now sits, and Glastonbury Tor that towers over it, was an island or a rounded peninsula joined to dry land by only a narrow neck of land. Archeological studies of the area reveal a civilization built on shifting sands. Entire townships were built on the swamp marshes that existed in this region at the time, linked by elaborate wooden walkways and bridges. When Joseph arrived at Britain, this is the land he would have found, and perhaps would have been familiar with. His first church, built for the continuation of Christ's teaching in this pagan land, would have been built in this context. Although it is debated whether the original wattle church, or "Old Church," would have been the familiar rectangular sanctuary or the primitive round houses more in keeping with the context, it is agreed that the early church would have had an appearance quite different from the Gothic ruins which we now know.

> During the British period worship would have been conducted in the Old Church, that is the venerable wattled structure which was later covered by planking and which was still standing in William of Malmesbury's day. This church would have resembled Irish buildings of the same era and may have been—in its later rather than in its original wattled state—nearly 60 feet long, just as tradition holds. Dr. Raleigh Radford points out, moreover, that the Old Church itself would probably not have existed in a vacuum and must be considered in the context of the whole island settlement [Carley, *Glastonbury Abbey*, p. 3].

Whatever form the original church would have taken, it served as the cornerstone for the huge cruciform abbey that was joined to this simple church. The original wattle church first stood as a Christian sanctuary in the wilderness. In later years, this original church was covered in wood planks and lead coverings to protect the old, venerated structure. From this state, the other churches, chapels, and structures that are outlined by today's ruins were added. When one looks at the classically medieval cruciform shape of the completed Glastonbury Abbey, it is easy to imagine the Grail held in the Old Church at the foot of the cross the abbey formed, just as the legend says it was held at the foot of the cross to collect the blood of Jesus Christ.

However, a tragic fate befell Glastonbury Abbey in 1184 when a fire caused by a candlestick touching a drape destroyed the abbey, including the original wooden Old Church. Although this was a devastating loss, full funding was soon granted for the dedicated rebuilding of the Abbey. When reconstruction was begun, one of the first duties to be carried out was to build a new chapel on the site of the Old Church. Today the ruins of the Lady Chapel, one of the most intact buildings left on the grounds, stand where the original wattle church stood before the fire. To commemorate this place, a brass plaque was mounted on a pillar to mark the Lady Chapel as the location of the Old Church, "lest the site or size of the earlier church should come to be forgotten."

It is quite easy to see that Glastonbury is a truly remarkable and holy site in Christendom. Its links to Joseph of Arimathea and the Grail make it something of a historical "conversation piece." However, in the long and curious history of Glastonbury Abbey, nothing has marked its place in legend quite like the discovery of King Arthur's tomb. Early Glastonbury history records that in 1191, presumably due to the reconstruction effort, a group of monks discovered the tomb, thanks to information given to them by a "Welsh bard."

First a stone slab was found seven feet down the pit. They discovered that a lead cross was affixed to the underside of this stone. The oddly shaped lead cross bore a Latin inscription that reads "HIC IACET SEPVLTVS IHCLITVS REX ARTVRIVS IH IHSVLA AVALOHIA." Although the form of this Latin is somewhat peculiar in places, it can be translated as "HERE LIES BURIED THE RENOWNED KING ARTHUR ON THE ISLE OF AVALON." Further down at an unusually deep 14 feet, the monks found two bodies entombed in what had been a large, hollow log or tree trunk. Since the bodies were male and female, and considering the cross they had found, the monks took the bodies from the pit and deduced that these were the bodies of King Arthur and his queen, Guinevere.

There is a period of uncertainty as to the whereabouts of the royal remains between the years of 1190 when the bodies were found and 1278 when they were reburied in a marble tomb under the High Altar, where the remains were open to viewing for a few hundred years. It is theorized that the bodies spent this missing time in the Lady Chapel, since this was the site of the Old Church. Ultimately the bodies were lost. However visitors to Glastonbury Abbey today can see signs marking both sites—the original tomb where the bodies and the leaden cross were found, and the site of the High Altar tomb.

SITE OF THE ANCIENT GRAVEYARD
WHERE IN 1191 THE MONKS DUG
TO FIND THE TOMBS OF
ARTHUR AND GUINEVERE

The site of King Arthur's grave, only a few yards south of the Lady Chapel at Glastonbury (John Koopmans).

This theory is substantiated when one considers Arthur's original association with Glastonbury. When Arthur ended his days at the battle of Camlaan, his story states that a brilliant vessel appeared to carry his earthly remains to the mystical island of Avalon, long thought to mean "Avaron," the name for the Celtic underworld. Considering Arthur's close ties to traditionally Celtic mythology, this conclusion at first seems most likely. However this may not be the case. Glastonbury has been called many things in its history, including Apalonia which means "Isle of Apples." This is quite close to "Avalonia," the word for Avalon both on Arthur's leaden cross and in many of his tales. To further justify this assumption, many Grail texts refer to a place called "Glass Island" which is the place where the Grail might be found, as well as the place where Arthur's body may be found. Since it is known that Glastonbury was originally called Ynys Witrin, meaning "Glass Island," it is most likely that Glastonbury is both Avalon and the "Glass Island" of Arthurian and Grail legends.

One may wonder how the body of the renowned King Arthur might have found its way to Glastonbury. This is in fact one reason why so many dismiss the account of Arthur and Guinevere's bodies being found there. It would seem strangely coincidental that these remains would be found in such close proximity to the center of the Grail legend. However, when one considers the death of Arthur in the context of the Grail at Glastonbury, the answer becomes clear. If Arthur sustained life-threatening injuries at his final battle at Camlaan, it would be reasonable that he would have been taken to Avalon/Glastonbury to be healed, where there was a tradition of healing administered by the cup of the Last Supper. In fact, later chapters will reveal a cup, found at Glastonbury, that is said to possess just such healing properties.

Although the discovery of Arthur's grave at Glastonbury is still in question, this site's place in the Grail legend is almost impossible to dispute. This is the place where Joseph brought his two vials of blood relics and founded his wattle church. There are in fact several places at Glastonbury Abbey, found around the old site of the Lady Chapel, that raise an eyebrow for those who are familiar with the Grail legend.

6

SECRET PLACES
OF GLASTONBURY

Although most accept Glastonbury as the center of Arthurian and Grail lore, many do not know of several interesting aspects of this already incredibly beautiful and complex abbey. One interested in the Grail legend will pay the most attention to the Lady Chapel, the site of the original wattle church built by Joseph of Arimathea. While the remainder of the ruins are beautiful in their own right, the small area which once held this wattle church seems the most mysterious—the most intriguing to the study of legend.

Here the investigation of Glastonbury turns again to the pursuit of the historical Grail. The lands of Glastonbury once measured twelve hides, one hide being enough land to sustain one man for one year. Recalling the tale of Saint Patrick coming to Britain, this exact amount of land makes perfect sense. When he arrived in the area of Glastonbury, he found a preexisting Christian community led by twelve men. They claimed they always had been led by twelve individuals, commemorating the original twelve who began the church at Glastonbury. Therefore, the original twelve hides of land which King Avaragus had given Joseph and his companions, as mentioned in the Domesday Book, were just enough to sustain Glastonbury's first settlers.

In John of Glastonbury's *The Chronicle of Glastonbury Abbey*, the tradition of Saint Joseph and Avaragus is mentioned again, along with another interesting connection to the Grail legend. The following

Inside the Lady Chapel looking eastward, with a ceremony being conducted in the lower level at Saint Joseph's Chapel (John Koopmans).

passage comes from section 14, entitled "ON THE SANCTITY OF THE CHURCH OF GLASTONBURY AND ITS CEMETERY, AND ALSO ON THE KINGS, BISHOPS, DUKES AND OTHER NOBLES BURIED THERE."

> Therefore a certain soothsayer of the Britons, Melkin by name, thus began his prophecy: "The Island of Avalon, eager for the death of pagans, at the burial of them all will be decorated beyond the others in the world with the soothsaying spheres of the prophecy, and in the future will be adorned with those who praise the Most High. Abbadare, powerful in Saphat, most noble of the pagans, took his sleep there with 104,000 men. Among these Joseph of Arimathea received eternal slumber in a marble tomb, and he lies on a divided line next to the oratory's southern corner where the wickerwork is constructed above the mighty and venerable Maiden, and where the aforesaid thirteen spheres rest. Joseph has with him in the sarcophagus two white and silver vessels, full of the blood and sweat of the prophet Jesus. Once his sarcophagus is discovered, it will be visible, whole and undecayed, and open to the whole world. From then on those who dwell in that noble island will lack neither water nor the dew of heaven. For a long time before the day of judgment in Josaphat these things will be openly declared to the living." Thus far Melkin. Also in this island of Avalon, which is called the tomb of saints, rest Coel, King of the Britons, father of St. Helen, the mother of the great emperor Constantine, and Caradoc, duke of Cornwall.

This idea of Helena being descended from British royalty appears to be a medieval misinterpretation. The *Catholic Encyclopedia*, in the entry for Saint (Empress) Helena Augusta, makes the following claim to explain the lack of historical evidence to support the above claim.

> It may arise from the misinterpretation of a term used in the fourth chapter of the panegyric on Constantine's marriage with Fausta, that Constantine, oriendo (i.e., "by his beginnings," "from the outset") had honoured Britain, which was taken as an allusion to his birth, whereas the reference was really to the beginning of his reign.

Although it appears Empress Helena was not born in Britain, it is true that Joseph's tomb was found in recent history, exposed when a heavy frost forced it up out of the ground. On this tomb there was another plaque inscribed which stated that this was the tomb of Joseph of Arimathea, and it went so far as to state that there at Glastonbury, Joseph came to rest after burying Christ in his own tomb. One might automatically jump to the skeptical conclusion that this is a hoax as many assume the discovery of King Arthur's tomb might have been. However, since Joseph's tomb was only discovered this century, it would have done little good to attract money-holding pilgrims willing to fill the abbey's coffers in the twelfth century.

The search for the Grail at Glastonbury is rekindled by remembering the earlier statement about Joseph's tomb. In John of Glastonbury's *Chronicle of Glastonbury Abbey*, we read that Joseph was entombed with "two white and silver vessels, full of the blood and sweat of the prophet Jesus." One would therefore think that the Grail, or in this case multiple Grails, were found in close proximity to their owner, Joseph of Arimathea. Unfortunately, this was not the case. There is no evidence that anything of this sort was found in the tomb, pushed out of the ground in the Glastonbury Cemetery, claiming to be that of the fabled Joseph of Arimathea. However, if we again reference the texts of the Grail legend, it would indicate that at least for some time, the tomb of Joseph was above ground in a place of veneration.

In one of the more obscure Grail texts, *Perlesvaus*, also known as *The High History of the Holy Grail*, the tomb is seen before the Castle of the Fisher King and will only open when the Castle is visited by the best knight in the world who will win the Grail. Knights come and go, but the tomb never opens. Finally Perceval comes before the castle and the tomb opens.

> Perceval cometh nigh the castle in company with his sister, and knoweth again the chapel that stood upon four columns of marble between the forest and the castle, there where his father told him how much ought he to love good knights, and that none earthly thing might be of greater worth, and how none might know yet who lay in the coffin until such time as the Best Knight of the world should come thither, but that then should it be known. Perceval would fain have passed by the chapel, but the damsel saith to him: "Sir, no knight passeth hereby save he go first to see the coffin within the chapel."
>
> He alighteth and setteth the damsel to the ground, and layeth down his spear and shield and cometh toward the tomb, that was right fair and rich. He set his hand above it. So soon as he came nigh, the sepulchre openeth on one side, so that one saw him that was within the coffin. The damsel falleth at his feet for joy. The Lady had a custom such that every time a knight stopped at the coffin she made the five ancient knights that she had with her in the castle accompany her, wherein they would never fail her, and

bring her as far as the chapel. So soon as she saw the coffin open and the joy her daughter made, she knew that it was her son, and ran to him and embraced him and kissed him and began to make the greatest joy that ever lady made.

We know this to be Joseph's tomb from another revelation made a few lines further down the text.

She maketh her chaplain take certain letters that were sealed with gold in the coffin. He looketh thereat and readeth, and then saith that these letters witness of him that lieth in the coffin that he was one of them that helped to un-nail Our Lord from the cross. They looked beside him and found the pincers all bloody wherewith the nails were drawn, but they might not take them away, nor the body, nor the coffin, according as Josephus telleth us, for as soon as Perceval was forth of the chapel, the coffin closed again and joined together even as it was before.

Might it be possible that if Joseph had with him, and was in fact entombed with, the Grail in the form of white and silver vessels, such vessels were removed for safekeeping at some time later? Since this tomb that was pushed up from its burial was not found to contain either of these vessels, it would make sense that these objects were removed at some time in the past, probably when the body was moved from an above-ground crypt to a below-ground tomb. It will become very important in future investigations of Joseph and his role in the Grail legend that such an object might have been held in safekeeping as a venerated relic.

Glastonbury Abbey today stands empty—a decayed memory of its old glorious history. With the exception of the annual flood of visitors, the abbey echoes only with the memory of a past that has made this little spot on the Somerset plain a truly legendary place. However, there is one small vestige of Glastonbury's remarkable, mysterious past which remains today in a place somewhat removed from the Abbey's ruins. In the Manor House of Nanteos, Wales, a very special object was once kept locked away in a cupboard until it was needed. Throughout its history, this nearly destroyed wooden cup has been known to have healed a number of people of ailments ranging from simple diseases to serious head injuries. What links this cup to Glastonbury is its history, specifically how it came to be at the Nanteos Manor. According to the Powell family who owns the cup, the Nanteos Cup was carried there by a group of monks from Glastonbury, fleeing the destruction of their own abbey with this cup, the Holy Grail, that had been safely hidden in the walls of Glastonbury Abbey.

The Nanteos Cup best fits our concept of what a cup from the Last Supper might have looked like. However, its most interesting history points back to the cradle of the Arthurian cycle and the legend of the Holy Grail—Glastonbury. Although the monks of Glastonbury Abbey claimed this was the cup that their founder Joseph of Arimathea had brought to Britain, traditional depictions of Joseph show him carrying two small containers, either flasks or small cruets, containing Christ's blood and sweat.

If the Nanteos Cup was hidden at Glastonbury, what evidence can be found to verify this claim? Unfortunately, there is little information about this cup itself. However, there is a great deal of information available about Glastonbury that lends itself to this cup's history. In fact, there are a number of points of interest, all found around the Lady Chapel, that invite investigation.

The Grail legend is exemplified by the legend of Joseph bringing the Grail to Britain after he and a small group fled Palestine after the crucifixion. One aspect of this legend is that Joseph hid the Grail in the well at Glastonbury. Most people believe this to be the Chalice Well—a well fed by a spring of iron-rich water, capped by an elaborately, symbolically ornamented well head. Found amid a beautiful garden at the foot of Glastonbury Tor, the Chalice Well is known for its role in Grail legend. The well head is decorated with a symbolic representation of the Holy Lance uniting the physical and the metaphysical worlds. The water of the spring runs red, also lending itself to the thought that the cup that held the blood of Jesus Christ might be found inside.

The problem with this well, and the idea that Joseph placed the Grail in it, is that the well itself apparently was not associated with the Grail until the mid-eighteenth century. Its place in Grail lore has been manufactured largely by those interested in the spiritual aspect of the Grail Quest. However, there is another well, more closely associated with Joseph himself, that is much older than the Chalice Well.

On the outer, south wall of the Lady Chapel is a well that appears to be quite old, possibly from Roman times. Called Saint Joseph's Well, it is accessed in two different ways. The easiest way is to request passage through a locked doorway found inside the Lady Chapel in the lower level, actually referred to as Saint Joseph's Chapel. This doorway leads through the southern wall and to the left to a small arch, decorated with

The ornate decorated cover for the Chalice Well near Glastonbury Tor (John Koopmans).

a somewhat primitive diamond pattern, over a simple hole in the ground—the well of Saint Joseph. The second method of access is via a curious, winding stairway that has been sealed off recently by the proprietors of Glastonbury Abbey for fear of visitors' injury.

Although little is known about this well, it is conjectured that it is fed by the same spring that runs through the Chalice Well. The archway over the well is considered pre-Norman, leading to the assertion that the well head was actually a window from a much earlier iteration of the church's construction. This well had been forgotten for quite some time until it was rediscovered in 1826 during the excavation of the Lady Chapel's lower level.

It is thought that the well's association with Joseph came from the resurgence of a cult centering on Joseph of Arimathea in the 1500s. Even if this is the case, the idea that the well was in some way related to Joseph must have come from a previous tradition. It is possible that this is the well in which Joseph placed the Grail. Although this well lends credence to the Joseph legend, it would seem unlikely that such an important relic would be simply cast down a well in the ground. It is possible that the idea of the Grail being hidden in the well is yet another confusion of the true history.

One of the other curiosities found on the south side of the Lady Chapel is the famous and enigmatic "Jesus/Maria" Stone, found approximately 24 feet further west of the well, roughly at eye-level. The meaning and origin of this stone have perplexed scholars and visitors alike for hundreds of years. Glastonbury historians assume the carving was made by a devoted medieval pilgrim, waiting in line to enter the Lady Chapel: however, this is most unlikely. Few other than scholars of this time could read or write, much less read or write Latin. Besides this obvious problem with the explanation, one would wonder who carried a full supply of stone-cutting tools on their person, and would they not be afraid of desecrating this holy site?

Many assume that the "Maria" of this stone refers to Mary, the mother of Jesus. Another possibility is that the stone refers to Mary Magdalene, the companion and disciple of Jesus who accompanied Joseph of Arimathea on his journey to Britain as far as France. Although the assumption that the stone refers to the Virgin Mary is justified in that the Lady Chapel is dedicated to her, the story of the Nanteos Cup may justify the Mary Magdalene theory. The story of the cup states that it had been hidden in a wall at Glastonbury for many years. Where else would it have been hidden than in the southern wall of the Lady

Passageway to Saint Joseph's Well, just outside the southern wall of the Lady Chapel (John Koopmans).

Top: Saint Joseph's Well (Francis Thye). *Bottom:* The Jesus/Maria Stone on the outside of the Lady Chapel's southern wall (John Koopmans).

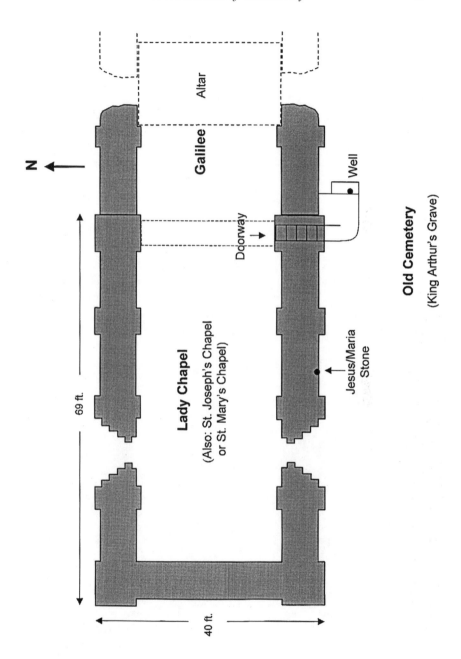

Floor plan of the Lady Chapel at Glastonbury Abbey. Note placement of the Jesus/Maria Stone and Saint Joseph's Well (John Koopmans).

Chapel in the same area as both the Jesus/Maria stone and the well of Joseph? Considering the proximity of the stone to the well, and the tradition that Joseph hid the Grail in, or possibly in the same place as, the well, the stone would seem to be a marker, much like the marker stone used to locate time capsules in modern buildings.

These hiding places establish a credible link between the Nanteos Cup and its alleged hiding place in the walls of Glastonbury. However, there is still the discrepancy between the cup as the Grail and the Grail as the two cruets brought to Britain by Joseph. While it is possible that the Nanteos Cup is in fact the Grail brought to Britain, numerous traditions concerning Joseph and the Grail always indicate that he brought with him, not one cup, but two small vials or cruets containing the blood and sweat collected after the crucifixion. It is therefore most likely that the Nanteos Cup is another relic entirely—the Marian Chalice.

The question of Joseph's cruets can also be answered at Glastonbury. In the lower level of the Lady Chapel, in what is called Saint Joseph's Chapel, there is a small crypt carved out of the ground and

The altar and crypt of Saint Joseph. The crucifixion carving is above the horizontal line of pale stone blocks and just under the peak of the arch (John Koopmans).

A close-up shot of the crucifixion carving behind the altar in the crypt of Saint Joseph's Chapel (John Koopmans).

encased in stone under what would be the entrance into the Galilee—
the room just beyond the Lady Chapel. Behind the altar, there is a stone
carving of the crucifixion which appears to be much older than the surrounding rock. Besides the beauty of the carving and its surroundings,
the truly fascinating thing about it is that there is a discoloration over
the region where Christ's heart would be. This stain is caused by the
kisses of thousands of faithful who have visited the site.

Again, little is known about this carving, but since it is clearly
quite old, and not in the Gothic style of the rest of the abbey, it is likely
that this stone is also a marker. This carving, like the Jesus/Maria stone,
is in a peculiar place. It could very well be that this carving marked the
spot where Joseph's cruets were once kept. Although the proprietors of
Glastonbury Abbey state that this stone was placed in relatively modern times, they concede to the fact that it probably came from an earlier placement. Regardless of where it originated, this stone was placed
in Saint Joseph's Chapel, indicating that it was likely associated with
Joseph prior to its present placement. It could have been a marker originally placed near the well; however, it is more likely that the carving
reflects the tradition of Joseph's role in the crucifixion. Therefore, this
stone may be marking the original location of Joseph's two cruets in the
small chapel.

There have been two relics that claim to be the real Holy Grail
that was brought to Britain by Joseph of Arimathea. One of these
objects is the Nanteos Cup as mentioned above, and the other is a pair
of vials allegedly interred with Joseph in his tomb. Since most think
there must be only one true Grail, one would assume that one of these
objects must be a fake or was at least mistakenly thought to be the
Grail. However, further investigation of the historical Grail may provide a different conclusion. Evidence is present to support both claims
validating these relics, thus linking them in some way to the true, historical Holy Grail. However, of these two relics with different origins
and equal claims of validity, which can rightly be called the Grail?

7

HOLY WARS
AND HERETICS

Along any Grail seeker's path of discovery, it is impossible to progress very far without running into a mysterious, and seemingly diabolical group from the Middle Ages called the Knights Templar. In fact, the study of biblical archeology is laced with references to the Crusaders and the Templars. While occupying the Holy Land, they conducted the first crude attempts at unearthing the past, albeit mostly concentrated on items of Christian importance.

History indicates that these sects were at first described as the finest example of European culture and bravery. However, the decline of these groups included allegations of offenses so severe that these groups of fine knights were excommunicated, and most were burned at the stake. How does one reconcile these diametrically opposed views of the Templars, especially in relation to the Grail mystery? It is clear that the greatest task in researching a historical mystery is to unlearn what has been learned, and separate historical fact from the machinations of man.

The four major Crusades took place between the years of 1096 to AD 1204, the most successful of which was the First Crusade, during which the Lance of Longinus was found in Acre, ending with the capture of Jerusalem in 1099. Although today the Crusades are viewed as a horrible, dark era in Western history, the Arab capture of Jerusalem was viewed with the same fear, anger, and indignation at the time as people in the United States would have viewed a Soviet attack during the 1980s.

In researching the Grail texts, the first of these heretical groups we recognize are the Knights Templar. These frugal, honorable, "Warrior Monks" began their brotherhood as protectors of the Western pilgrims, journeying to the Holy Land during the Crusades. Along this path lay many dangers—attacking forces, robbers, thieves, assasins, and the enemy of the Crusading Europeans, the Turks.

The Knights Templar were known for their generosity and frugal nature, their emblem being two knights riding on one horse. However as the Crusades continued, the Templars also became known for their power, wealth, and skill at finding and possessing Christian relics of great importance. With their increasing power and wealth, they became a dangerous challenge to the Roman Catholic Church.

As the objective of the Crusades was to recover the Holy Land from the Saracens, so it seems was the purpose of the Knights Templar to find relics of Christian importance. The first such discovery was made when the Crusaders conquered the city of Acre in upper Palestine. As legend states, the invading knights prayed for strength before their upcoming attack on Acre during the First Crusade. As if in answer to their prayers, there was a vision of a shining cross standing over the site where the Lance of Longinus rested. With this vision as inspiration, the knights overtook Acre and there discovered, under a chapel floor, what they thought was the Holy Lance that belonged to Longinus, the Roman centurion who pierced Christ's side at the crucifixion. Many medieval and crusade historians have stated that this discovery served as an impetus for the remainder of the Crusades.

Another mysterious object that is said to have been discovererd by the Knights Templar is the Ark of the Covenant. A group of Templars built their base at the site of the Temple Mount in Jerusalem and remained there for several years. The Templars were said to have spent their years there excavating the site which was once the location of King Solomon's Temple that housed the golden Ark of the Covenant. The Bible states that the Ark was there for many years and then suddenly disappeared. It is conjectured that the Ark was either moved from the palace, or most likely hidden there on the Temple Mount itself, just before the destruction of the Temple by the Babylonians in 586 BC. One possibility which is commonly accepted throughout modern Masonic Templar circles is that the Templars discovered the Ark of the Covenant during their encampment on the Temple Mount, and that it is currently hidden away in the catacombs under Rosslyn Chapel in Midlothian, Scotland, near Edinburough.

Of all other items allegedly discovered by the Templars, without question the most well known of those would be the Shroud of Turin. After their misguided sacking of Constantinople in 1204, the shroud cloth was taken and came into the possession of Geoffrey de Charny around the year 1350. For many years under the threat of excommunication and the weight of financial difficulties, the keepers of the shroud battled the Roman Catholic Church over their right to claim its ownership. Although the Shroud of Turin was moved to its final sanctuary in the Royal Chapel of Turin Cathedral in 1694, it was passed from family to family, until 1983 when it was finally left to the Vatican by Italy's last king, Umberto II of the House of Savoy.

One very interesting aspect of the Shroud legend may be a vital link to the allegations which proved to be the Templars' downfall. The Shroud of Turin was first displayed in Edessa in the form of a long rectangular reliquary called the "Mandylion." The only way to see the relic was through a circular opening in the ornate lattice covering. Clearly visible through this opening was the image of a head, specifically the ghostly image of Christ as seen on the shroud today. Although we may now see the full, and in fact doubled, image of Christ on this shroud, the only image that was thought to be in existence at that time was this image of Christ's head.

This leads us to the decline and fall from favor of the Knights Templar. With the power, numbers, and wealth of the Templars constantly growing, the Church began another type of holy war, only this time it was against its former perfect knights. The accusations flung at them included homosexuality, witchcraft, and advocating of the overthrow of the Roman Catholic Church. However, the most damning claim was that their secret rituals worshipped the devil himself in the form of a head called "The Baphomet." This head was supposed to be a truly hideous depiction of Satan in his most gruesome form.

It is not difficult to conclude that most of these charges were either largely fabricated, exaggerated or outright lies when one considers the context of the Inquisition. In fact, most researchers would now agree that the head Baphomet was most likely the Shroud of Turin again in its folded, Mandylion form. It is well known that the Templars claimed to have been in possession of many holy relics such as this and held them with the highest reverence and care. It is most likely that these charges were levelled at the Templars simply because they posed a political threat to the Church.

We might say the same of the other allegedly heretical sect known as the Cathars. The Cathar belief of the duality of good and evil and the path of personal spiritual enlightenment began around the second century AD. They separated themselves from the Roman Catholic Church, claiming their beliefs were in accordance with much older traditions than those held by the Church, dating back to the early Christian church. The Cathars were centered in the Languedoc region of southern France, around the cities of Albi, Toulouse, and Carcassonne. However, when one mentions the Cathars to anyone familiar with their tale, only one name comes to mind—Montsegúr.

Pope Innocent II began what is known as the Albigensian Crusade against the Cathars for their obvious heresy against the Church. The Cathars resisted the domination of the Papacy and retreated to several fortified castles in their region. The last of these castles to fall was Montsegúr. After ten months of seige and starvation, the Cathars of the castle Montsegúr resigned themselves to defeat. After a short time in which they were allowed to renounce their beliefs and swear devotion to the Roman Catholic Church, they refused to deny their doctrine and were burned at the stake.

This would be an otherwise tragic but unremarkable event in medieval history and in relation to the Grail legend if it were not for one fact. Being closely linked to the Knights Templar, the Cathars were also said to possess many treasures and relics of great value, not the least of which was the alleged cup of the Last Supper. This was in fact their greatest object of reverence, and possibly the very core of their teaching.

Legend states that the night before castle Montsegúr fell, four Cathar brothers descended from the wall surrounding the castle and stole away in the dark of night, carrying what they claimed to be their greatest possession, very likely the Grail. No one knows any more than this about the legend of the Grail at Montsegúr with the exception of two very important facts. The first is that when the armies entered the ruins at Montsegúr, they found no trace of the revered chalice, despite an almost frantic search. The second indicator is found in the caves beneath the castle. Although no written account of the Grail or the Cathars who fled with it can be found there, one can in fact see a large, cryptic painting of a Grail-cup deep inside one of these caves.

Although both the Templars and the Cathars were seen as heretical and were accused of many crimes against Christianity, their appearance in the Grail legends paints them as anything but loathsome and unholy. In fact, whenever a Grail text portrays the Templars, they are always seen as the keepers of the Grail and other holy objects.

The dual nature of the Templars as heretics and humble priests is seen in the Grail text, *Perlesvaus*. There they are portrayed as a curious band of monks who are seen to beat a wooden cross, and then to revere it with great sadness. When the Grail hero of this text sees the group of monks, he is first compelled to confront such an act of disrespect for the Holy Cross. However, he is told not to disturb them in their ministrations. Immediately afterwards, the monks adorn the cross and pray piously at the foot of the cross as if it were an object of incredible worship. All this is later explained to Perceval by a hermit in the woods. He said that this group beat the cross because it was the source of such pain and suffering for Christ, but worshiped it because through it all men gained salvation.

Rosslyn Chapel in Midlothian, Scotland, is seen as one of the most highly revered places in Freemasonry and in the Grail legend nearly equal in acclaim to Glastonbury and Montsegúr. This chapel was built by Sir William St. Clair in 1446, and it was only the beginning of what was intended to be a much larger cruciform church typical of the period.

The most remarkable feature of Rosslyn Chapel is the obvious meeting of several different and outwardly contrasting traditions. Stone carvings of Christ being judged before Pontius Pilate stand near a pillar ringed by the serpents of creation from Norse mythology, Celtic Green Men peek out of every corner, angels hold the heart of Robert the Bruce, crusader and subsequently the first true King of Scotland, and most mysteriously, carvings of corn native to North America decorate archways long before the first recorded journeys to the New World. It is clear that Rosslyn is a truly sacred, yet mysterious, place.

> Rosslyn Chapel is the Third Day of Creation in stone. It is a rebuilding of the Temple of Solomon carved within its luxuriant friezes of plants and leaves and flowers. It was also built as a Chapel of the Grail with the Knights of the Grail buried in its vaults [Sinclair, p. 63].

This place has been a haven for the scattered remains of the Knights Templar since their dissolution, and it has also housed pieces of some of the most sacred relics in Christendom. One may find in Rosslyn a darkened cross adorned with silver, which is said to be an exact replica of another cross which once contained a piece of the Holy Rood, the True Cross. It is possible that the fleeing Cathars discussed previously may have retreated to Rosslyn, known to be the place where the most valuable holy relics could be safely kept hidden. If this is true, we may also assume that they carried with them their precious Grail-cup.

This theory is further supported by the symbology found in Rosslyn and on the tombstones around the area. The Sinclair (St. Clair) family symbol is that of a thorny cross surrounded by a shield—an "engrailed cross." A similar engrailed cross can be found on the tomb markers of the Templars buried in the surrounding area. Along with the common theme of the calipers, compasses, and right-angle squares of the Freemasons, there is the engrailed cross in the form of a Rosy Cross, surrounded by a circle, supported by a long stem, ending in a stair-stepped base which is supposed to represent the steps leading up to the Temple of Solomon.

It has been alleged that the Templars and Cathars have had in their possession the Grail, the Ark of the Covenant, and a piece of the True Cross. This presents a view of these "heretical" sects which appears anything but sacrilegious. Beyond this, Wolfram von Eschenbach as well as many other Grail text authors portrayed them as the guardians of the Grail. What else might serve as evidence to prove their relationship with the Grail?

Many people are familiar with the typical tools of "divination." Among these are the crystal ball, tea leaves, and palm readings. However, the most well known of these items reaches far beyond the entertainment value of carnival fortune tellers and New Age mystics. The cards of the Tarot deck have been used for years for such purposes. Regardless of one's view on the subject of divination, this peculiar forerunner of the modern deck of playing cards might shed some light on these heretical sects and their role in the Grail legend.

The Tarot deck is commonly accepted as being such a tool of fortune telling devised by Gypsies—their knowledge originating from Egypt. However, actual historical records indicate the existance of Tarot card decks as long ago as the mid-1300s, near the time of the writing of *La Folie Perceval* in 1330. Although what is known as the Minor Arcana is mostly similar to a modern deck of cards (a two through a ten, three "face" cards of a King, Queen, and Jack, and sometimes a Joker), the other cards of the Tarot known as the Major Arcana hint at a purpose more significant than simple amusement.

The four different signs, or suits, of the Minor Arcana are the Cup, Sword, Rod, and Pentacle or disk. These suits are quite similar to the items known as the Grail Hallows—the Chalice Cup, the Sword which beheaded John the Baptist, the Lance of Longinus (which is similar to a rod), and the Dish or platter, which is identified either as an object used at the Last Supper or the plate on which the head of John the Baptist was brought to Salome. These hallows are depicted in a manuscript illustration from *La Folie Perceval* which will be discussed in the next section. The Grail in the form of a Ciborium is first, followed by the lance, ending with the Sword which beheaded John the Baptist on top of a covered box containing the plate of the Last Supper.

The card that links the common deck of playing cards, the Minor Arcana and Major Arcana, is the "Joker" card. This card is very much like the "Fool" card in the Major Arcana of the Tarot Deck. While this card is usually the first card in a standard deck of playing cards, it is also the first card of the Major Arcana.

Since the word "Arcana" stems from the word "arcane" which simply means "hidden" or "lost," this further leads to the notion that these cards were meant not for divination, but for illumination—teaching a now hidden or lost philosophy. While such a philosophy is well outside the bounds of this text on the Grail, and largely a matter of personal beliefs, its relevance to the Grail legend is clearly illustrated in a little-known Grail text entitled *La Folie Perceval*.

As Graham Phillips outlines in the eleventh and twelfth chapters of his book *The Search for the Grail*, this seldom-read text might have stemmed from an earlier work known as the *Peveril*. The interesting link between the Grail and the Tarot deck lies in the characters who Perceval, the first, most traditional Grail hero, encounters along his journey.

Commonly described as the "Perfect Fool," Perceval himself can be seen as the first card in the Major Arcana, "The Fool," the card meaning "folly" or "carelessness." The second character Perceval meets along the way is the Red Knight, who later turns out to be Merlin the Magician in disguise. This corresponds to the second card in the Major Arcana, "The Magician," the card meaning "skill" and "diplomacy." Next Perceval meets a wise woman who tells Perceval where he may find the Castle of the Fisher King. This enigmatic individual corresponds to the card of the "High Priestess," the card meaning "secret," "mystery," and "wisdom." Oddly, Phillips continues to describe how there has only been one female "Priestess" or Pope in the Roman Catholic Church, namely Joanna Aquila, or "Joan the Eagle"—a similarity made all the more mysterious by the words she uses to tell Perceval who she is. She states, "I am an eagle who flew higher than any who dwelt in Rome."

The procession of the Major Arcana through the *Folie* continues with the figures of the Fisher King and his Queen since the third and fourth cards of the Tarot are "The Empress" and "The Emperor." The fifth card of the Major Arcana shows up next, not in person, but in the haunting, fateful words that keep Perceval from asking the all-too-important question about the Grail. The fifth card is "The Hierophant," which has a meaning of one who has good intentions, but misguides. This is an appropriate description since the Old Knight who helps instruct Perceval in the ways of knighthood before his meeting with the Fisher King gives his foolish student misguided advice when he tells Perceval not to ask many questions for risk of appearing irritating.

Here the procession continues, but in a less orderly manner. Perceval next encounters a hooded figure he assumes to be a monk, but who turns out to be Death. Perceval then finds himself again in the company of the wise woman, described as "The Priestess" above. However, these things soon fall into place when Perceval encounters a pair of lovers sitting under a tree, identified with the sixth card in the Major Arcana, "The Lovers." It is followed soon thereafter by the seventh card, "The Charioteer"—a giant from whom he must obtain a Golden Apple. The Charioteer is also seen to be holding a bleeding lance, obviously identifiable with one of our Grail Hallows.

Then, the ninth card of the Major Arcana, "The Hermit," shows up in the form of the ever-present hermit of the forest whose purpose in these Grail stories is to explain the strange things that have been happening to Perceval and provide important visions. After the hermit comes the hooded figure who represents the thirteenth card, "Death."

When Perceval finally finds the Grail castle, it has been reduced to a burning ruin by a lightning bolt sent by the devil. In keeping with our chain of events, the fifteenth and sixteenth cards of the Major Arcana are respectively "The Devil," then "The Tower," which is depicted as a castle tower being destroyed by a lightning bolt.

Finally Perceval finds the Rich Fisher King again and asks the important question, "Whom does the Grail Serve?" Perceval then sees the Grail, only this time it is as a sacred book, which shines so brightly Perceval cannot at first read from it, although the Fisher King can view it quite easily. When Perceval accepts his role as the new Guardian of the Grail, he too can read from the book. This brightly shining book can be seen as the seventeenth card, "The Star," which has a meaning of "hope and promise for the future."

The nineteenth card is present in the form of another old tale from the Arthurian saga. Most Arthurian students are familiar with the story of Sir Gawain and the Green Knight or Sir Perceval and the Red Knight in which a deadly challenge is made. In each case, an unfamiliar knight offers the chance for a knight of Arthur's court to deal him a blow with a weapon which will clearly take the unknown knight's life. When the death blow is taken, it is discovered that this mysterious knight is enchanted and can survive the strike. In exchange, the knight from Arthur's court must agree to return in one year to receive his blow in like manner. Such an agreement is made in *La Folie Perceval* between Perceval and the Red Knight.

After Perceval becomes the new Guardian of the Grail, the Red Knight stabs Perceval through the body with his sword, returning the blow which Perceval promises to take after one year. However, as the new, immortal Fisher King, Perceval cannot die, and honor is satisfied without death. This sequence is represented by the nineteenth card of the Major Arcana, "The Sun," which has a meaning of "contentment" or "completion."

The twentieth card, "The Last Judgement," can also be seen in this event. This card, both in the image on the card and in its meaning, means "renewal," "rebirth," and "triumph over death."

The story ends aptly with the last card of the Major Arcana, "The World." This card, which represents the "New Jerusalem" or the "Kingdom of Heaven," matches what happens in the *Folie*. At the end of this Grail story, Perceval builds a new Grail castle, and a white maiden takes the sacred book into heaven.

It is certain that these cards and the story of *La Folie Perceval* have some very clearly indicated similarities. Although not every card is present, this omission could be the result of missed hints due to the interpretation of a lost tradition, or the editing and rewriting done by those transcribers who preserved this text.

The Templars and Cathars have been portrayed as "heretical," but in truth they might have been the keepers and protectors of a most holy object. The Templars were described as the Knights of the Grail in more than one text, as well as in the history of the Rosslyn Chapel. The Cathars fled with what they thought was the Grail before they were captured at Montsegúr. Lastly, the Tarot deck, which appears to have originated with the Cathars and was used as a tool for teaching their beliefs, is almost exactly reproduced in one Grail text which appears to have been based on one of the oldest Grail texts in existence—possibly the originating text for both the *Mabinogion* and Chrétien's tale of Perceval and the Grail.

Now, we enter the realm of ancient history, medieval myth, and true archeology. From here, we must try to understand the relics of Christ's Passion which were found by the Templars and by other people throughout history. By learning more about them, we will be able to understand more about the nature and history of the more elusive relic known as the Holy Grail.

8

RELICS

During the Middle Ages, and especially after the Crusades, relics of Christ's Passion allegedly were prolific. In fact, one might say there was an overabundance of such relics. Some scholars of the medieval have stated that if all the "authentic pieces of the True Cross" were actually authentic, they would produce a cross taller than the the Eiffel Tower. This concept of the fabrication of relics is by no means a modern one. Geoffrey Chaucer wrote of it in the Prologue of his *Canterbury Tales*. He spoke of a certain member of their group of pilgrims—a Pardoner of the Roman Catholic Church.

> But in his craft, from Berwick unto Ware,
> Was no such pardoner in any place.
> For in his bag he had a pillowcase
> The which, he said, was Our True Lady's veil:
> He said he had a piece of the very sail
> That good Saint Peter had, what time he went
> Upon the sea, till Jesus changed his bent.
> He had a latten cross set full of stones,
> And in a bottle had he some pig's bones.
> But with these relics, when he came upon
> Some simple parson, then this paragon
> In that one day more money stood to gain
> Than the poor dupe in two months could attain.
> And thus, with flattery and suchlike japes,
> He made the parson and the rest his apes [lines 694–708].

Chaucer here describes how such pardoners, whose job it was to "sell" pardons and other religious items such as relics of the Saints, sold falsified relics to local churches and other individuals on a regular basis. Although this was common practice during the Middle Ages, it does not negate the validity of all items which currently exist as relics. In fact, some items which currently reside in chapels, cathedrals, and museums were discovered so long ago that they predate the medieval practice, and in fact predate the Roman Catholic Church. To fully understand the Holy Grail as a historical object, a relic, in other words, one must investigate the relics of Christ's Passion that exist today, as well as some other ancient items of biblical importance.

This investigation must begin with what may be called the first relics to be discovered by the Christian West. The first Roman Emperor to accept Christianity did in fact make it the national religion. Constantine the Great converted to Christianity, as legend states, due to a miraculous vision just before entering a great battle. He prayed to his gods for strength, and in response, Constantine witnessed a great, glowing cross in the sky supported by four cherubim. Trailing out from the cross was a banner which read, "BY THIS SIGN YOU SHALL CONQUER." Constantine and his army immediately accepted Christianity and proceeded to defeat his opponent with astounding success.

In the year 327, his mother Empress Helena Augusta journeyed to Jerusalem in an effort to locate the places associated with Christ's Passion. She soon discovered what she felt to be the garden tomb of Jesus covered and masked by a temple to the Roman god Jupiter. After entering the tomb, she found several objects that were supposedly used during the crucifixion, not the least of which was the True Cross accompanied by the crosses of the two other men crucified along with Jesus.

As legend states, the titular board nailed to the cross over Jesus's head (which read IESVS NAZARENVS REX IVDORVM—JESUS OF NAZARETH, KING OF THE JEWS) had come off the cross, making the cross of Jesus indistinguishable from the other two. Therefore, she had a sick and dying woman brought to the tomb, where she proceeded to touch the first, then the second cross with her hand, resulting in no change in her state of languor. Finally, she was made to touch the final of the three crosses. Upon touching the wood of this cross, the woman became instantly revived and jubilantly walked away from the tomb.

While no one can validate the claim of such miraculous cures as set down by this legend, it does perpetuate the concept of items being found inside the tomb. This tale is intimated in the early medieval poem "The Dream of the Rood," in which the wood of the cross is first cursed for the pain it caused Christ to endure, and then revered for being the instrument of His resurrection and mankind's salvation.

However, the cross was not the only item Helena found inside the tomb, merely the most famous. Many of the other relics of Christ's Passion are supposed to have been found by Helena in the tomb. These include the nails used during the crucifixion, the titular plaque, the pincers used to pull out the nails, the sponge used to give Christ the drink of wine and vinegar on the cross, the Crown of Thorns, the Lance of Longinus, and according to the account given by Olympiodorus as mentioned earlier, a small cup which is referred to as the Marian Chalice.

These items, commonly called the "Arma Christi," or Instruments of the Crucifixion, are depicted in many medieval paintings and illuminations, variously including the items mentioned above, more items present in the story of the crucifixion such as the dice the Romans used to gamble over Christ's clothing, and sometimes the relics from other saints such as the head of John the Baptist. However, the one object mentioned above which is not present in any of these paintings is the cup.

While these paintings were seen as sacred themselves, not subjects for interpretation as would be most other paintings, the discrepancy among the various images depicting the Arma Christi demonstrate that some license has been taken with the actual objects shown. Examples of this include the Mandylion, which was supposedly not included in Helena's findings. Other discrepancies include the fact that the jars used to transport the large amounts of perfumes and precious oils used during the preparation of Christ's body are seldom included although they are clearly mentioned in the Bible.

Of all the items which were claimed to have been found by Helena in the tomb, the only one which has very specific, written historical proof was the one item never present among the Arma Christi—the Marian Chalice. If all these items found in the tomb are authentic, where are they now? Where would they be sent for worship, protection, and for posterity? To determine this, we must learn more about each individual relic.

As stated above, the cross was found inside the tomb of Jesus by Helena, along with the other articles of the Crucifixion. After finding these objects, Helena sent a sizable portion of the cross to Constantinople, along with two nails, to be received by her son, Constantine the

Great. There, he placed a small piece of the cross inside a statue he had made of himself which supposedly was to make Constantinople unconquerable. He also took the two nails and included them in the making of his helmet and his horse's bridle.

Besides these pieces of the cross, several other segments have found their way to other sites throughout Europe, including tales of a piece being held in the Rosslyn Chapel for many years. However one of the most interesting histories comes from the pieces left behind in Jerusalem.

At least one of three large segments of the cross remained in the Church of the Holy Sepulchre, built on the exact site where Empress Helena Augusta found the tomb of Jesus, the building of which was commissioned by Constantine himself. Here it was hidden for many years to guard it against unscrupulous relic hunters. However in AD 614, King Chosroes II of Persia invaded and ransacked Jerusalem, taking hundreds prisoner, as well as the piece of the sacred cross.

King Chosroes took this segment of the cross in its golden, bejewelled reliquary to his mighty palace, the Throne of Arches, or the Takt-I-Taqdis. Its dome was decorated with jewels to reproduce the constellations in the night sky, and it was said to rotate on wooden rollers and a giant spoked wheel powered by many beasts of burden beneath the palace. It sat on a solid foot of black obsidian, appearing like a great black lake. This description of King Chosroes's Takt-I-Taqdis sounds a great deal like the "Turning Castle" described by Albrecht von Scharffenberg, the thirteenth-century poet, in his "Der Jungere Titurel." It is thought that Scharffenberg made the assumption that, along with the piece of the True Cross, the Persian king may have taken the Grail as well.

However, the Cross was not to remain long at the Takt. In 629, the Byzantine emperor Heraclius overtook and destroyed the Takt, reclaiming the cross and other spoils stolen from the Holy Sepulchre.

Although almost every large church and cathedral throughout Europe is said to hold a piece of the True Cross, the most widely accepted fragments can be found in the Vatican, Notre Dame Cathedral in Paris, Oviedo Cathedral in Spain, and the Cathedral of Ghent in Brussels.

The nails of the crucifixion, which consisted of the three large nails used to afix Christ to the cross as well as one or two smaller nails used to attach the titular plaque over Jesus's head, are claimed to be housed in many different locations of importance throughout Europe. Although most of these are either not authentic, fragments, or reproductions used for purpose of veneration, the most noteworthy nail relics can be found in Notre Dame Cathedral along with the cross fragment and the Crown of Thorns, and in the Cathedral of Santo Croce in Jerusalem which also claims to possess one-third of the titular plaque in an elaborate gold reliquary. This segment of the plaque was discovered by a group of workmen in 1492 behind a red stone slab upon which was written "HIC EST TITULUS CRUCIS—HERE IS THE TITLE OF THE CROSS."

The true nature of the Crown of Thorns is a bit debated. While most Western art depicts it as a ringlet of vine-like stems, bristling with long, straight thorns, most people who study the plant life of the area have a different opinion. The 1978 Shroud of Turin Research Project, or S.T.R.P., asserts that the crown was not a circlet at all, but was instead a type of cap which covered the whole head, only ending in the painful, prickling spines at the points of the leaves. This theory is supported by the following passage.

> The crown is mentioned as having been found in the Holy Sepulchre. Cassiodorus (c. 570) spoke of the crown being at Jerusalem: "There we may behold the thorny crown, which was set upon the head of the Redeemer." St. Gregory of Tours (d. 593) asserts that the thorns of the crown still looked green, a freshness he said that was "...miraculously renewed each day" [Cruz, p. 35].

Here the crown is said to appear green, not brown or black as the typical crown is depicted. The plant which is thought to have been plaited together to form the crown is named "Zizyphus Spine Christi," an assessment which has been confirmed by more than one study.

It is theorized that the crown as we now have it is simply the portion that fit around Christ's forehead. While the most intact segment of the crown that remains and forms this circlet is in the Notre Dame Cathedral, almost one hundred spines can be found scattered throughout sites in Europe, the most notable of which are the Cathedral of Trier in Germany, and the Oviedo Cathedral in Spain.

The cloth relics of Christ's Passion are perhaps the most mysterious and widely debated objects in existence. Although the Shroud of Turin is the most famous among these, other cloth items of equal importance include the "seamless" vestment over which the Romans gambled at the crucifixion, and the face cloth or "Sudarium" used during the preparation of Christ's body for entombment.

Although little is known about the seamless vestments of Christ, one thing is quite clear. For the Roman centurions to value the clothes of a Jewish heretic enough to gamble for them, the quality of the vestment must have been quite extraordinary. These were no common man's clothes. They would have been fine enough to rival those worn by the magistrate himself. The custom of the time was to divide the crucified man's clothing, often tearing it into separate pieces. However, legend states that when the soldiers saw how unusually fine this vestment was, they decided to cast lots for its possession.

The face cloth or Sudarium is said to be the cloth which covered Christ's face as his body was being prepared for burial in the tomb. The cloth measures roughly 32 inches long by 20 inches wide, and it is made of tightly woven linen, stained mostly in the center by blood and water. St. John's Gospel mentions a cloth other than that of the Shroud which was said to have been "rolled up in a place by itself." Although the markings on this cloth very closely resemble those on the face areas of the Shroud, its history is quite different.

> Its history is known, and is different from that of the Shroud. The Sudarium stayed in Jerusalem until AD 614, when it began to be moved from place to place just ahead of conquering Persian armies. It was taken first to Alexandria in north Africa, from there to Cartagena in Spain, then to Toledo, and from there finally to safety in the Cathedral of Oviedo, where it has been kept without interruption since the mid-eighth century [Whanger and Whanger, p. 56].

As mentioned, the Sudarium may have a very different history than the more famous Shroud of Turin, but the stains which cover its center area have been shown to match the blood stains present on the Shroud quite closely. Doctors Alan and Mary Whanger, co-founders of the Council for Study of the Shroud of Turin, or C.S.S.T., and inventors of the Polarized Image Overlay Technique, have actively researched the Shroud of Turin since 1979, producing some of the most stunning findings ever discovered.

The Whangers studied the faint images and stains on the Shroud for many years, paying very close attention to detail. As a result, they have discovered imprinted images of many objects on the Shroud such as numerous flowers and bouquets, the nails of the crucifixion, the pliers used to remove the nails, the titular plaque showing some of the lettering, the sponge on a reed, the crown of thorns, the spear, and a broken head phylactery which contains tiny scriptural verses from the Torah.

These findings are not easily dismissed. Pollen analysis has been conducted on the Shroud for years, indicating the presense and indeed abundance of plants and flowers found only in Palestine, several of which grow only in the area around the site now identified as Calvary. The pollen findings have led other botanists familiar with the plant life of the area to do further research on the evidence of flowers and plants on the shroud. Independent research has also found the outline of individual flower petals and leaves on the Shroud. Although the S.T.R.P. group who conducted an in-depth study of the Shroud could not come to a definite conclusion on its validity, such corroborated findings would certainly indicate that it is indeed what it claims to be, not a medieval forgery.

The Shroud has been safely housed in the Cathedral of St. John the Baptist in Turin, Italy, since 1578, and it is now permanently unrolled in its hermetically sealed glass enclosure. Although public viewings are rare, Shroud researchers say that it is now in much better condition than it has been in the past, the constant rolling and unrolling, handling, and polluted air having been factors damaging the already faded image on the Shroud.

Although the Shroud of Turin and other relics beg a lifetime of investigation, they must now be left for later study. Attention must now be turned to the alleged relics that have more relevance to our current study of the Grail legend. There are many cups to chose from—many stories and histories. However, some relics play a larger role in the Grail legend than others. The Grail is actually a part of a larger cache of items that are usually seen together in Grail texts. The Grail Hallows, as they are called, include one relic that is considered as holy as the Grail itself—the spear that pierced the side of Christ.

9

THE SPEAR OF DESTINY

The Spear or Lance of Longinus is without question one of the most revered objects among the Arma Christi. It is both a sacred relic and a legend in itself, as seen in several Grail texts. It is also one of the four Grail Hallows, almost as important as the Grail itself. In fact, depending on what you take to be the authentic spear, it may be two of the Grail Hallows—the spear and the sword that beheaded John the Baptist. This point may be quite confusing; however, it takes only a cursory reading of the lance's history to learn that there is more than one lance claiming to be that used to pierce the side of Christ.

Legend states that the blind Roman centurion, Longinus, pierced Christ's side on the cross to hasten His death since the Sabbath was quickly approaching. When a drop of blood dripped into his eyes, his sight was instantly restored. Longinus is also identified with the Roman soldier who at the foot of the cross made the statement, "This is truly the Son of God."

Although the spear is one of the objects supposedly discovered in the tomb, it would at first seem unlikely that a Roman centurion would give his spear for the burial of a Jew. In fact, a Roman losing his spear for any reason was a grave offense, punishable by death. However, if one considers Longinus's statement acknowledging Jesus as the Son of God, it is possible that he chose to become Christian or to pay some small homage to Christ—giving his blood-covered spear for the burial to honor the Hebrew tradition. To learn more about the spear that pierced Christ's side at the crucifixion and which was later found in His tomb, a greater understanding of the spear's history is necessary. When one begins to investigate almost any aspect of the Arthurian/Grail legend, the first discovery made is that not one but several candidates quickly arise, claiming to be the one true article. History demonstrates that the lance is no different.

Present in both the Arma Christi and the Grail Hallows, the spear begins its journey through legend at the crucifixion. However, after this originating point, the spear seems to fracture and become many different objects. The spear and other articles of Christ's Passion were discovered in the tomb of Christ when Empress Helena Augusta uncovered Christ's tomb in Jerusalem. Thereafter the spear and other holy articles were kept safe in Jerusalem despite Hadrian's attempt to destroy all Christian relics in AD 135. This is confirmed by the written account of Antoninus, a sixth century pilgrim to Jerusalem, who saw the lance hung in a place of reverence in the Church of the Holy Sepulchre.

Here it remained until AD 614, when Jerusalem was sacked and many of these holy items were removed by the invading Persians. However, when Emperor Heraclius reclaimed these items from the Persians, he returned the lance to Jerusalem. Wishing to have a piece of this relic for himself, however, he took the lance's tip, which had been previously broken off, to the Chapel of Pharos in Saint Sophia's in Byzantium.

Although this is the first mention of the spear's fracturing, the confusion of multiple lances began right after its discovery in Christ's tomb. When Helena found the Arma Christi in the hidden tomb, some of these relics were immediately divided. Although the lance was not divided at this point, its saga was made all the more confusing by the nails found in the tomb. Helena sent three of these nails to her son Constantine. He used two of the nails in the making of his crown and his horse's bridle. However, the third was used to make a second lance that was a replica of the first he used to mark off the boundaries of Constantinople.

With Constantine's use of this spear, the idea of the lance as an instrument of divine power took on a life of its own. The spear underwent a transformation from Christian relic to a talisman of right to leadership. This sentiment was forever cemented when a lance, claimed to be that which pierced Christ's side, fell into the hands of Charles Magnus, the soon-to-be king. The Pope gave Charlemagne the spear 25 years before he became king. Despite its definite seventh century form, the Pope claimed that this lance, now called the Lance of Saint Maurice, was the lance carried by Constantine containing nails from the True Cross.

After Charlemagne's crowning as king in AD 800, the lance was used as a symbol of power and divine right to rule. Not surprisingly, several different lances cropped up around Europe after Charlemagne's death. However, the dark chapter of the spear's history that would begin its fame as the "Spear of Destiny" was only just beginning. King Henry, ruler of the lands that would become Germany, sought to find relics of the Passion to legitimize his rule, the most powerful of these relics being the lance. After his death, the lance passed to his son, Otto I. To further splinter the spear's history, Otto had two copies of the lance made, which he gave to the kings of Hungary and Poland.

This spear, handed down through the rulers of the Holy Roman Empire, used as an object of power, then began to undergo another change—almost a backward mutation from talisman to relic. Seeking to legitimize this lance as the one true lance of the crucifixion, Otto III placed nails in the spear, which he claimed were nails from the Arma Christi. After Frederich II moved the lance to Nuremberg in 1250, where it would remain for 550 years, King Charles IV made an engraving on the collar joining the halves of the spear, which had by this time been cut in two. The engraving stated that these were the true lance and nails used during the crucifixion.

This lance very well could have become the most widely accepted relic had it not been for another discovery made by Crusaders at Antioch. In 1097, Crusaders began their siege of the city of Antioch, far north of Jerusalem. Their battle to overtake the city continued until 1098 when a young spy showed them a secret way into the city. However, their victory was short-lived. A new Muslim army soon arrived, threatening to take away what they had fought so long to gain.

Near the point of breaking, new hope was brought to the Crusaders in the form of a dream. One among them said that Saint Andrew appeared to him in this dream, pointing the way to the resting place of the lost lance of the crucifixion. Led to the basement of St. Peter's Cathedral, soldiers dug under the floor stones and did indeed find an ancient lance. Although this discovery would serve as a rallying point among the Crusaders there and throughout Europe, a Papal ambassador among their company had seen the Lance of Longinus some years before in Jerusalem. He wisely chose to remain silent.

The validity of this lance was immediately brought into question when the Crusaders offered the lance to the Emperor of Constantinople. The Emperor already had what he believed to be the true lance, but he chose to take the gift anyway. Following this discovery, the

Armenian Christians found out about this new lance, and claimed they had possessed the true lance for many years. In what appeared to be an attempt to cover all possibilities, all of these other lances were taken to Constantinople.

The safety of these lances soon ended, however, when the Crusaders overtook Constantinople in 1204, and all of the secondary lances held there became the trophies of King Baldwin II. These confused, forgotten relics might have ended in obscurity had they not been sold to King Louis of France in 1241. All the other lances of Constantinople, and the tip of the original lance of Jerusalem, were then housed in the magnificent reliquary of Sainte Chapelle in France.

Of the other spears claimed to be the true lance, little is known. The lances of Constantine and Antioch were lost, the original lance remained in Constantinople, and the tip of the original lance as well as the Holy Roman lance remained in France until the French Revolution. In 1453, the original lance was taken from Constantinople by invading Turks. However, this lance was recovered when Pope Innocent VIII struck a bargain with the Turkish Sultan who held the lance. The relic would be returned to the Pope in exchange for the Sultan's brother who was at the time being held prisoner. Upon the lance's return, it became the property of the Vatican where it is currently enshrined in one of the four great pillars at Saint Peter's Basilica.

Although the lance that is most widely accepted as the true relic of Christ's Passion is that hidden in the Vatican, the lance of the Holy Roman Empire would continue to make its mark on history in the centuries to come. The Holy Roman Empire fell with the French Revolution, and what remained of the once great world force became the responsibility of the Hapsburgs of Germany.

In 1205, Wolfram von Eschenbach composed his Grail epic *Parzifal* that would serve as the inspiration for Richard Wagner's opera *Parsifal*. This story, glorifying the power of the lance, opening in a time of diminished national pride and increased interest in medieval romances, became quite popular in the Germany of the young Adolf Hitler. After a failed attempt to begin a career in art, Adolf Hitler attended a performance of *Parsifal*. In the opera's adoration of the lance, Hitler found a cause and the impetus for rekindling the once glorious flame of the Hapsburg's Holy Roman Empire.

In 1938, Hitler rode into Vienna to take the spear from the Hofburg Museum in Vienna, Austria. This began an almost surreal attempt to re-create the Grail legend in the Third Reich. Heinrich

Himmler envisioned a royal court of high ideals using Arthur's court as a model and the Grail Quest as a theme. Although Himmler wanted to take possession of the lance for his endeavors, he was only given one of many copies of the lance that Hitler had made. The Lance of Saint Maurice was then taken to Saint Katherine's Cathedral where it had rested originally during the Holy Roman Empire.

However, due to Hitler's ever-increasing paranoia, the Lance wound up in a secret, underground vault under Nuremburg Castle. It was here, on April 20, 1945, where General Mark Clark discovered the lance after the fall of the Third Reich and the suicide of Adolf Hitler.

On the 7th of January in 1946, the Lance of Saint Maurice was returned to the Hofburg Museum where it can be seen today. Copies of this lance remain in Hungary and Poland. The lances of Antioch and Constantine were lost. The Armenian lance is still considered a cultural treasure. All that remains of the original lance is enclosed in the pillar at the Vatican, and the tip was moved from Sainte Chapelle to the Bibliot Nationale during the French Revolution. As an interesting footnote to the lance's intriguing history, Pope Benedict XIV sent an emissary to Paris to have a drawing made to scale of the tip from the original lance. Upon returning the drawing to Rome, the Pope found that the lance and the tip depicted in the drawing once formed one contiguous piece.

The spear used at the crucifixion most likely would have been a type of six-foot-long throwing and thrusting spear called a "pilum." This spear of the crucifixion, to accomplish its goal of piercing Christ's side, would have been long and thin, probably with a small tip, much like a pilum. Although the relic at the Hofburg Museum is quite likely not the spear of the crucifixion, or possibly not even a spear at all, it would not be likely that such a revered object could simply be a forgery. Although it does not appear to be the blade from the Spear of Longinus, it does bear a striking resemblance to another weapon of a Roman Soldier—his sword.

If one looks at the typical ornamental dress of the Roman centurion, one of the most common things found would be his sword, the Gladius. Athough it took the appearance of a typical short sword in the later empire, the original Gladius, used around the time of Christ's crucifixion, looked slightly different. It was roughly the same length as its later form, but the tip was more elongated and tapered more gradually, making a much sharper point. Although this description is very similar to the object found in the Hofburg Museum, the most stunning similarity is seen in the blade's shape. Halfway down the blade, the original Gladius curved inward on both sides making what is called a "wasp-waisted" profile, much different than the later Gladius. The object in Vienna has nearly the exact same shape and size of this Roman Gladius. If one imagines this spear in one piece, without its golden collar, without its embedded nails, with an added Gladius handle (a large, round pommel, with a finger-grooved handle and a semispherical hilt), the transformation becomes complete. The Spear of Destiny becomes an original Roman Gladius.

What could be the explanation for this erroneous identification of a Roman Gladius sword with a Roman centurion's spear? Taking inventory of the Grail Hallows, one sees the Grail cup, the dish of the Last Supper, and the Spear of Longinus. However, there is another item not associated with Christ at all, but with John the Baptist.

> And when a convenient day was come, that Herod on his birthday made a supper to his lords, high captains, and chief estates of Galilee; And when the daughter of the said Herodias came in, and danced, and pleased Herod and them that sat with him, the king said unto the damsel, Ask of me whatsoever thou wilt, and I will give it thee. And he sware unto her, Whatsoever thou shalt ask of me, I will give it thee, unto the half of my kingdom. And she went forth, and said unto her mother, What shall I ask? And she said, The head of John the Baptist. And she came in straightway with haste unto the king, and asked, saying, I will that thou give me by and by in a charger the head of John the Baptist. And the king was exceeding sorry; yet for his oath's sake, and for their sakes which sat with him, he would not reject her. And immediately the king sent an executioner, and commanded his head to be brought: and he went and beheaded him in the prison. And brought his head in a charger, and gave it to the damsel: and the damsel gave it to her mother [The Holy Bible, King James Version, Mark 6:21–28].

The sword used to behead John the Baptist is the fourth and final Grail Hallow. Since it now seems unlikely that the relic in the Hofburg Museum is the spear, it is possible that it could be this sword.

At this point, one must answer two questions that further confuse the nature of the Hallows. Why is this sword so closely associated with the objects of Christ's crucifixion as depicted in the paintings of the Arma Christi?

John the Baptist has always been very closely associated with Jesus Christ, from the message of his ministry to his baptizing of Christ.

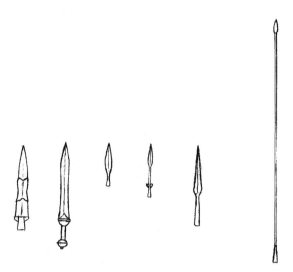

From left to right: The Spear of Destiny, a Roman Gladius, various spear points, a Roman pilum (the author).

Even in the womb, Jesus and John appeared to be closely linked. After the angel's annunciation to the Virgin Mary that she was to conceive a child who was to be named Jesus, she goes to visit her cousin Elizabeth, who she discovers will soon have a child herself, to be named John.

> And Mary arose in those days, and went into the hill country with haste, into the city of Judah; And entered into the house of Zacharias, and saluted Elizabeth.
> And it came to pass, that, when Elizabeth heard the salutation of Mary, the babe leaped in her womb; and Elizabeth was filled with the Holy Ghost:
> And she spake out with a loud voice, and said, Blessed art thou among women, and blessed is the fruit of thy womb. And whence is this to me, that the mother of my Lord should come to me? For, lo, as soon as the voice of thy salutation sounded in mine ears, the babe leaped in my womb for joy [The Holy Bible, King James Version, Luke 1:39–44].

It is clear, both from Biblical reference and from the history of the early church, that Jesus and John the Baptist were very closely associated.

Therefore, it should not be surprising that such a relic of John the Baptist should appear as one of the Grail Hallows.

There is considerable evidence that the so-called lance in the Hofburg Museum in Vienna is not the Lance of Longinus, or even a spear at all, but a Roman Gladius, missing its handle, which has been made to look like a spear head by later relic hunters. In light of the sword's inclusion among the Grail Hallows, this Gladius was most likely preserved as a relic because it was the same sword used in the beheading of John the Baptist.

The sword is clearly listed among the Grail Hallows. There may even be references to this notion in the Welsh *Mabinogion* in the tale *Peredur*. One may recall that the Grail in this story was not a cup at all. It was the severed head of Bron the Blessed, a living oracle kept animated in a bowl full of blood. This image of the head and bowl is quite reminiscent of John the Baptist's story. One can imagine the head of John the Baptist idealized in the early Christian mind as an oracle resting in a salver filled with its own blood which was the ancient Hebrew seat of the soul.

Since *Peredur* and other Welsh tales have produced pagan images of objects related to Christ's Passion, the head of Bron the Blessed might have been representative of John the Baptist's head resting on a salver in a pool of its own blood. This notion may be at odds with the popular idea that the Grail legend was simply derived from Celtic mythology. However, one must consider the possibility that if Joseph arrived in Britain a few years after the crucifixion, as evidence would indicate, these early Christian events would have been told to the indigenous peoples living in Britain at the time. Therefore, their stories of these events would be much the same, only with their own cultural ideals heavily influencing the basic nature of the events being retold.

It is therefore clear to see that John the Baptist and the sword used in his beheading figured prominently in the Grail legend and its associated texts, both from the Christian aspect and apparently from the Celtic aspect as well. For this reason, the relic housed in the Hofburg Museum, shaped more like a Roman Gladius than any type of spear point, is much more likely the sword used to behead John the Baptist than the lance used to pierce Christ's side at the crucifixion.

Now that the historical nature of the Grail Hallows has been made more clear, the last act of understanding the Grail legend is simply to discover the true nature of the historical Grail. There are several vessels around the world that have been claimed to be the Grail, but which claim is valid, and is there only one? Again the question is asked, "What is the Grail?"

10

HISTORICAL GRAIL
CANDIDATES

The search for the Grail has now come full circle. As Perceval is required to ask, the question must now be put forth again. What is the Grail? As is the case with most other Christian relics, Europe is full of objects claiming to be the real thing. However, the mere fact that there are many vessels that would be called the Grail does not discount, or even blemish the belief in or study of, a historical Grail. Each potential Grail has its own story to be researched and its own history to find. Similarly, each theory has its own claims that must be validated or discounted. It is clear to see that the study of the Grail is no easy task. To determine the true nature of the object at the center of this two-thousand-year-old mystery, it is necessary to learn about the objects which today claim to be the one true historical Grail.

In recent years, several books have been written about the Grail which take a somewhat unorthodox but historical approach to the Grail legend. Referred to as the "Holy Blood" books, the theory is introduced to the legend that the Holy Grail is actually no physical object at all. Instead, they claim it to be a lost or hidden bloodline—a lineage, beginning with a union between Jesus and Mary Magdalene which begat the great empires of Western civilization, ending with the modern-day descendents of the Templars, the Freemasons, being the sole holders of this long-lost knowledge.

The evidence cited is thought provoking, to say the least, outlining how the Merovingian Empire rose to power, thanks largely to being part of this hidden bloodline. The theory states that this lineage is a fact hidden throughout time in the mysteries of cryptic symbology, ancient rites, and the expansive Rennes le Château mystery that spreads across the landscape of France. It references such intriguing sources as the Dead Sea Scrolls, apocryphal texts, and lost gospels of the Bible, including the Gospel of Thomas, that is thought to have been written during the lifetime of Jesus. For further information regarding these theories, books such as *Holy Blood, Holy Grail* by Michael Baigent, Richard Leigh, and Henry Lincoln; *The Bloodline of the Holy Grail* by Laurence Gardner; and *Key to the Sacred Pattern: The Untold Story of Rennes-le-Château* by Henry Lincoln are recommended.

Although a modern discussion of the Grail would surely center on this theory, thanks mostly to its current popularity, this is but one idea among many about a very old legend. Some say the Grail is the Ark of the Covenant, others say the Grail is the womb of the Virgin Mary since she was the receptacle of Christ's essence. A recent theory makes the assertion that the Grail is actually the Shroud of Turin since it was found in the tomb and had absorbed a portion of Christ's blood. These are to say nothing of the New Age thoughts regarding the Holy Grail.

While the Holy Blood theory is provocative, it is simply that. The theory appears based largely on the dubious assertions of a power-hungry empire seeking to legitimize its rule. While there may well have been a great deal of mystery and encryption of secret doctrine involved in Rennes le Château and many medieval religious sects, these are all the creations of man, attributed to the Grail legend long after any of the events which founded the legend took place. The claim of the Merovingians is little different than the popular medieval claim among English kings to have been descended from King Arthur himself.

The most widely accepted explanation for the Grail's appearance in medieval literature is attributed to an act of plagiarism. Many well-known Grail researchers such as John Matthews maintain that *Le Conte du Graal* was an almost exact transcription of another, supposedly earlier work of Celtic folklore entitled *Peredur*, as found in the Welsh *Mabinogion*. This book, a compilation of several Celtic tales passed down through the spoken word only, contains the same story of Perceval, here called Peredur, who sees three knights riding through the forest, traveling to King Arthur's Court, only now the Grail is a bowl containing the severed head of Bron the Blessed.

To most, this is an obvious example of a practice common to the early Christian church. Pagan sites, traditions, and holidays were "restructured" to reflect a Christian theme, allowing early converts to more easily accept Christianity. Several churches throughout Britain are built on the sites of Celtic sacred circles, and many holidays, such as St. Valentine's Day, were older Roman or Greek holidays which were altered slightly to maintain the preexisting tradition, and to fit in with the tenets of Christianity.

While the Celtic Grail seems quite likely, one needs only to scratch the surface of the theory to see its flaws. The *Mabinogion*, on which the connection between the Grail and Celtic mythology rests, includes stories that are old indeed, but *Peredur* is not one of them. The first part of the book holds the oldest texts, while *Peredur* can be found near the end, along with other texts which can only be dated to near the time of Chrétien's now-famous text. While it may be that *Peredur* and Chrétien's Grail text came from the same source book, this does not preclude a physical, historical Grail.

In fact, most of the Celtic texts which seem to support a Celtic Grail date back only to a time near that of Arthur in the sixth or seventh century AD. Since tradition and historical reference indicate that Joseph of Arimathea came to Britain in the first century AD, these texts would have been written centuries later, dating from a time nearly as distant as Columbus's landing in the Americas is to us today.

If one looks further back than these, to an age near the time of Christ or before, all we find are Celtic tales of mystical cauldrons, exhibiting only the slightest likeness to our Grail as we have it. While Celtic vessels such as the Ardagh Chalice, Glastonbury Bowl, and the Gundesdrop Cauldron are beautiful and richly ornamented, as one would expect an object of reverence to be, this alone does not make them likely candidates for the historical Holy Grail.

If these facts do not settle the question of a Celtic Grail, there is one fact which may have been forgotten. The previously mentioned reference to the Marian Chalice, made by the Greek historian Olympiodorus, an accepted and reliable source for historical information, leads the researcher to a conclusion far removed from the Celtic tradition. If the Grail was simply a Celtic forgery, why was the reference made to the cup found by Empress Helena Augusta in Christ's tomb, and why was it sent to Britain, a land set at the very heart of the traditional Grail mystery? Could it be that the idea of the Grail as a Christian relic was not influenced by Celtic mythology, but vice versa? Might it be possible that the Celtic tales of Arthur's search for a magic cup or bowl were originated by the arrival of a Christian relic on the British Isles?

The Chalice Well Cup

The "father" of the Grail saga, Joseph of Arimathea, was said to have come to Britain with his small band of followers, carrying the two small cruets of Christ's blood and sweat. The legend states that upon reaching the top of Wearyall Hill, Joseph thrust his staff into the ground, and it immediately erupted into bloom and leaf—a sign of the divine nature of this, their new home. The Grail he carried was supposedly hidden in a natural spring at the foot of Glastonbury Tor.

There is in fact a well fed by a natural spring near Glastonbury, appropriately named the Chalice Well. The water of this well has stained the rocks over which it issues blood red, and it is said to have the metallic taste of blood. Those who have investigated the well also claim that there is a slightly elevated level of radiation coming from the depth of the well. Although a cup was allegedly discovered inside the well through a fantastic sequence of clairvoyant "visions," there is little evidence to support such claims regarding the Holy Grail being hidden in the well before the nineteenth century.

Rosslyn Chapel and the Apprentice Pillar

Grail researcher Trevor Ravenscroft, who wrote extensively about the Spear of Destiny and Hitler's interest in it, also made the assessment that the Grail was hidden away in Rosslyn Chapel in Scotland. He claimed the Grail had been hidden away inside one of the most elaborately decorated pillars in the chapel—the Apprentice Pillar.

The story of this work of art is a familiar one among Freemasons. Supposedly the pillar was designed by a master stonemason, intended to be his finest achievement. However, while the master was away, his apprentice took the plans and created the pillar himself, far surpassing the skill and beauty defined by the original plans. When the master returned, he beheld the exquisite beauty and surpassing skill with which the pillar had been made, and in a fit of rage he killed the apprentice with a sharp blow to the crown of his head.

The theme of this story is a fundamental tenet of all Masonic orders. The student must eventually surpass the teacher, thus dying as a student to be reborn a master. Such are the grades or orders of Freemasonry. To become a Grand Master, one must first progress through a series of learning steps, completing each with a ceremonious "death" to proceed to another level.

While Rosslyn Chapel does indeed boast an incredible history, filled with the hint of relics and great holy guardians, the only proof to demonstrate the Grail's existence in the Apprentice Pillar came from a metal detector test. A scan of the pillar did seem to indicate a metal mass which would be suitable for a metal cup. The only problem with this theory is that no shape was determined and could have been almost anything metal, not necessarily the Grail. To make matters worse, the curator of the historical site refused to have the pillar examined with an x-ray. In fact any archeological activity other than a simple external investigation has been met with the greatest resistance.

The Sacro Catino

This peculiar vessel, found during the First Crusade, may be the strangest of our contenders to be the historical Grail. However, it may have been an influential force on some of the later "alchemical" treatments of the Grail legend.

This octagonal green Roman glass vessel, once thought to be a bowl carved from a single emerald, measures 14 inches across the lip, and is a flat bowl rather than a chalice. Discovered after the capture of Caesarea, this enigmatic object was simply "said to be used at the Last Supper." Although this claim has little historical justification, the Sacro Catino does have one feature which mirrors a magical characteristic of Wolfram's Grail. In his *Parzifal*, he claims the Grail is actually the "Lapis Excillis," the emerald stone that dropped from Lucifer's crown as he fell from heaven. Besides possessing the magical powers of healing and the giving of rich feasts, the Lapis choses its own protectors—their names magically appearing inscribed on the stone. The Sacro Catino, which was also thought to be made of emerald, does have inscribed on the rim very fine writing which is only visible under certain lighting.

This artifact of the Grail legend sits on a wrought-iron tripod stand in the Treasury of San Lorenzo in Genoa, Italy. Although its picture cannot be taken for further study, it holds its secret silently amid the cracks of the ages and much rough handling. Although this potential Grail has a fascinating history, there is again little reason to think it is anything other than a Roman artifact to which there have been applied too many magical, alchemical allusions.

The Great Chalice of Antioch

Currently held in The Cloisters of the New York Metropolitan Museum of Art, this exquisite work of silversmithing begs investigation by anyone interested in the Grail legend. The great cup is surrounded by an elaborate lattice work of grapevines which contain many tiny sculptures of the Apostles as well as two depictions of Christ—one as a young boy and one as a man. Although this beautiful piece of work is what truly brings the story of the Grail to mind, it in itself is simply an ornate overlay which serves as a reliquary. The much simpler inner cup is thought to have come from the first century AD. Found early this century along with the smaller, "lesser" chalice of Antioch, a cross, and two book-cover plates of stenciled silver, this chalice fits the profile of other types of Roman chalices used around the time of Christ and was the subject of the 1954 movie, *The Silver Chalice.*

Since this large chalice was discovered in Antioch, its dating has been challenged. It was first said to have originated in the first century, though it is now accepted that the cup dates from the fourth century. Although this chalice was obviously created as a glorification of Christ and the Last Supper, it is both not old enough and too large to be the cup of the Last Supper. It has been theorized that the Great Chalice of Antioch may be the preserved relic of a wine jug or an amphora which contained the oils presented for Christ's entombment; however, this is only supposition.

The Cathar Grail at Montsegúr

Here begins what may be called the "short list" of the most likely contenders to be the Grail. As stated previously, the Cathars at Montsegúr fled with an object they described as their most precious holding before the castle fell. Besides having a rich tradition surrounding the Cathars, southern France has another tradition surrounding Mary Magdalene.

Mary, one of the company of Joseph of Arimathea which departed from Palestine, came to the Sainte Baume and Sainte Maximin regions of southernmost France where she is said to have spent her last 30 years with her brother Lazarus and her sister Martha. After her death at Sainte Maximin, her relics wound up in Vézelay where they have been safely housed since the early fifth century. The most interesting feature of this story is that among the relics found in the discovery of her tomb, there was an alabaster flask containing the blood of Christ.

Considering the proximity of her tomb to the infamous ruins of Montsegúr Castle, it is quite likely that the Grail with which the four Cathars escaped capture was in fact this alabaster flask which once belonged to Mary Magdalene. This flask is the first encountered in this study of possible Grails which both claimed to have once held the blood of Christ and belonged to someone who was present during the preparation of His body for entombment. Furthermore, the theme of the flask containing the sacred blood is one that will soon become more important.

It may be unclear at first how a flask can be called the Grail. Most think of the Grail as the cup used at the Last Supper. Although this may be true, the Grail is much more than just this. One must remember the statement made earlier that the Grail was more than one object. In fact, it can be justly said that the Grail itself is nearly as splintered as its tale. To clearly understand the remainder of this book, it is necessary to suspend the notion that the Grail is simply the cup of the Last Supper that caught Christ's blood at the crucifixion. Suspend the thought that the Grail is simply one object. One must instead think of the Grail in terms of its characteristics—a cup from the Last Supper, a vessel that held Christ's blood, a relic said to have belonged to Joseph of Arimathea, Nicodemus, and Mary Magdalene. The truth of the Grail legend is that the legend doesn't tell the whole truth about the Grail.

11

THE SANTO CÁLIZ
OF VALENCIA

The Santo Cáliz (Holy Chalice) of Valencia has the auspicious honor of being the only modern-day contender for the title of "Historical Grail" that has the Vatican seal of approval, although not as the Grail per se. It is, however, considered an authentic relic by the Vatican, and it has been used during holy celebrations and in the Eucharist by many popes throughout modern history.

When one first sees the Santo Cáliz, the immediate sense one may get is that this ornate, bejewelled golden Eucharist chalice could in no way be the cup from which Christ drank at the Last Supper. Was Christ not a proponent of a simple life, shunning such worldly riches? Would not such a cup be plainer than this, perhaps made from clay or wood? The answer is yes—this chalice is far too ornate to be the cup of the Last Supper. However, if one is familiar with the concept of a "reliquary," the explanation becomes quite clear.

A reliquary is a highly ornate and decorative cover or container in which the simple relics themselves are kept. For example, the Crown of Thorns in Notre Dame Cathedral is shrouded in a beautiful golden reliquary, offering only a circular window through which one may see the actual crown. In the case of the Santo Cáliz, the base, neck, and handles that form the reliquary appear more utilitarian, making the actual relic appear somewhat diminished. This might lead to some confusion over the simplicity of the chalice's bowl, which is the actual relic. The

The Santo Cáliz of Valencia (Catedral de Valencia).

gold and jewels are found only on the bottom portion of the chalice that forms the reliquary.

While the neck, base and handles are made of gold, containing a total of 27 pearls, 2 rubies, and 2 emeralds, the cup itself is quite simple. The bowl or cup of the chalice is made of a type of agate called "Oriental Cornerina" and is dark red in color. The base and all of its rich decorations were added only in the thirteenth and fourteenth centuries during its time spent in the secret mountain monastery of San Juan de le Peña.

The cup existed as a cherished relic for hundreds of years, as records would indicate, even as far back as the time of Christ. An investigation of this chalice reveals a truly rich history that forms the most complete, most often cross referenced, and most contiguous historical guide to a cup claiming to be the Holy Grail.

The history of the Santo Cáliz states that after the death of Christ, the disciple Peter took possession of the cup after it caught the blood of Christ. He then carried it with him in his missionary travels to Antioch, and later to Rome. Here the rich tradition of the Cáliz as the first chalice of the Eucharist begins. The next 23 popes followed in Peter's tradition of using it for the giving of the sacrament.

The Santo Cáliz was used in Mass for approximately 200 years, until the time of Pope Sixtus II. During this time of Christian persecution, in which Roman Emperor Valerian began executing all church bishops and priests, the cup passed hands from Sixtus to Calixtus to St. Laurence who finally hid it to ensure its protection. Just before St. Laurence's death, a Roman soldier was given the cup with orders to take it to Huesca in Spain. Along with the cup, the soldier was given a remission letter that read, "Please give this to Orencio and Paciencia," who were the priests of the church at Huesca. The Santo Cáliz remained there until 713 when, during the Muslim invasion of Spain, the cup was taken by the bishop Audeberto to a cave in a mountain called "Pano" near Jaca. Once there, he met a hermit named Juan de Atares who helped him found the secret monastery of San Juan de la Peña.

In Ean and Deike Begg's book, *In Search of the Holy Grail and the Precious Blood*, San Juan de la Peña is described as "a place of refuge for the Christian religion in Aragón during the Moorish occupation" (p. 108). The book continues to state that here Don Alfonso the Battler began his unsuccessful attempt to reconquer Spain in 1104, making his "proto-Templar knights" swear an oath of Holy War before this Grail. After his death at Fraga, he later bequeathed his kingdom to the Knights Templar. Here we see our first historical connection between the legendary guardians of the Holy Grail, the Templars, and the Grail itself.

The Santo Cáliz remained here in the monastery of San Juan de la Peña, during the time in which Chrétien de Troyes penned his famous *Le Conte du Graal*, until 1399 when King Martin I the Humane of Aragón removed it to the Royal Palace of Zaragoza. In 1424 it was moved again, this time to the Palacio de Real in Valencia by King Alfonso V the Magnanimous. Finally, King Alfonso's brother, King Juan I of Navarra, had the Santo Cáliz moved to its final resting place, the Catedral de Valencia, where it can be seen today.

An interesting aside to the chalice's history, pertaining to the creation of the jeweled base, was discovered by a member of the Confraida del Santo Cáliz, Juan C. Gorostizaga. As found in the 1990 book *El Santo Grial: Su Historia, su Culto, sus Destinos* by Juan Angel Oñate, one theory is that the base of the Santo Cáliz was made from another cup entirely. Oñate claims that the base could be the chalcedony agate cup of Sultan Abulfat Mahomet of Egypt who claimed it was the cup of Christ from the Last Supper. Then in 1322, this cup was purchased from the Sultan by the king of Valencia and Aragón who sent it to the Royal Palace of Aljaferia in Zaragoza. According to this theory, it is when King Martin the Humane took the carnelian agate cup from the Monastery of San Juan de la Peña to the Royal Palace that it and the Sultan's cup were joined and adorned to form the Santo Cáliz as it is seen today.

Regardless of whether or not this part of the cup's history is true or false, there is one part of the story of the Santo Cáliz that does not ring true. A cup cut from this rich stone would not have been found among the tablewares of any typical Hebrew household. Therefore, the Santo Cáliz of Valencia would not fit the description of a cup of the Last Supper in this sense. Stone was usually used to make vessels that would contain perfumes or oils, such as those used during funerary preparation.

Although the Santo Cáliz would not appear to be the type of cup found at the Last Supper, it would indeed fit Western culture's concept of the Holy Grail as described by Chrétien de Troyes. Since it was venerated by the Proto-Templars at the hidden monastery of San Juan de la Peña, it would be understandable that the Templars would have continued in the tradition of protecting and venerating this sacred relic.

John Paul II kisses the Santo Cáliz (Catedral de Valencia).

Tabernacle of the Santo Cáliz (Catedral de Valencia).

An important link between the Templars and the Grail legend can be found in an investigation of Chrétien's sourcebook. Wolfram von Eschenbach claimed that this book, and indeed the original Grail story, were derived from a mysterious person named Kyot. Scholars who study Templar history and Grail texts seem confident that the person of Kyot is actually Guiot de Provence who was both a troubador and apparently an initiate in the Templar teachings. It is quite interesting to find how Guiot is related to both Wolfram and Chrétien.

> Guiot is known to have visited Mayence, in Germany, in 1184. The occasion was the chivalric festival of Pentecost, at which the Holy Roman Emperor, Frederick Barbarosa, conferred knighthood on his sons. As a matter of course the ceremony was attended by poets and troubadours from all over Christendom. As a knight of the Holy Roman Empire, Wolfram would almost certainly have been present; and it is certainly reasonable to suppose that he and Guiot met [Baigent, Leigh, and Lincoln, p. 294].

The significance of this reference is seen earlier in this passage. The town of Toledo, Spain, the area from which Guiot originates, was a center for scholarly learning, especially in Muslim and Judaic studies. One must recall that the court of Mary of Champagne was also a center for such studies. Therefore, it is just as likely that Chrétien and Guiot met at this gathering, presumably as did Wolfram. However, if Chrétien did not meet Guiot at this festival, it is likely that such learning was shared between the two courts.

Links between Guiot and Wolfram are made all the more intriguing by one specific aspect of Wolfram's Grail. Eschenbach describes the Grail as an alchemical stone, on which there is a secret inscription that outlines the names and lineage of each member of the Grail family. The Santo Cáliz has just such an enigmatic inscription on its base. Written in Cufic Arabic, it has been interpreted as "For the most flourishing." However, due to the unusual character of this lettering, there are several other interpretations which include, "For whom flourishes," "For who is the flowering," "The flowering town," "Glory to Mary/Mary's Son," and "The Merciful" (a Muslim term for God). One other interpretation of this engraving is "Albst Sijs" which reads "Al-labsit As-Silis." This interpretation, when read aloud, sounds very much like "Lapis Excillis," the term used by Wolfram von Eschenbach to describe his alchemical Grail in *Parzifal*.

In the history of the Santo Cáliz, one can see an almost perfect, unbroken chain of events leading from its origin to the Cathedral of

The painting *El Salvador* by Juan de Juanes, showing Christ with the Santo Cáliz of Valencia (Catedral de Valencia).

Drawing of the inscription found on the bottom of the Santo Cáliz of Valencia (the author).

Valencia where the Confraida del Santo Cáliz guards it and educates interested individuals about it today. It isn't difficult to see why the Vatican honors it as the most probable candidate for the Holy Grail. There is only one aspect of its history that seems unrealistic—its claim to be a cup from the Last Supper. It has been seen that the Last Supper would have been a simple affair.

The Passover meal, or Haggadah, was a meal to commemorate the compassion of God for His people and was thus conducted in a humble manner. It is therefore unlikely that the trappings of the meal were anything other than plain, even in the event of a holy man visiting the house in which the Last Supper was held. With that in mind, it is hard to imagine a beautiful agate cup, even devoid of its beautiful reliquary, being used instead of a plain wooden or ceramic cup or bowl. It was rare that people of this meager social standing had in their possession anything greater than this, except possibly a few pieces of Roman glasswork.

However unlikely this may be, it is even less likely that Peter, the patriarch of the Roman Catholic church, would have taken a vessel of no importance away from Palestine and made it the first cup of the Eucharist. Investigating the nature of the original agate cup, one comes to find an interesting piece of information that might have quite an impact on the Cáliz's case as the historical Grail. The agate from which the cup is made is described as "Oriental Cornerina"—*oriental* being the key term. According to research on the early history of the cup itself, it was cut from a single piece of agate in Egypt sometime between the fourth and the first centuries BC.

This fact may lead back to another connection to our first Grail story and to the "father" of the legend, Joseph of Arimathea. As a metal merchant, he would have visited several shores around the Mediterranean. If these travels went as far from home as the Cornish coast of England, they surely would have included Egypt. In fact, biblical historians have postulated that Jesus, Joseph, and Mary's flight to Egypt would have required the assistance of someone familiar with or perhaps even living in that area. Since it has been demonstrated that Joseph was probably related to Mary and Jesus, it is quite likely that Joseph of Arimathea would have accompanied Mary, Joseph, and Jesus during their flight to Egypt since he surely would have previously traveled there, buying, selling, and trading for goods and materials.

One may see further evidence of this by returning to the mysterious Shroud of Turin. Research has shown that the cloth is of a weave unlike that native to Jerusalem—a pattern more like that found in Egypt, specifically in mummy wrappings. If Joseph traded for goods in Egypt, he very likely purchased there the items he wanted used for his own burial, including the shroud and other items such as the agate cup.

It is clear that the cup atop the Santo Cáliz was most likely too rich in quality to be used as a simple drinking cup or bowl at a meal intended to demonstrate humility. All things considered, it would be much more likely that this agate cup would have been intended for a more ritualistic purpose—a vessel intended for Joseph of Arimathea's own burial which was instead used for the burial of Jesus, along with Joseph's own new tomb and shroud.

Here in this unlikely place, the one chalice that was most likely the Holy Grail as described in the Grail texts has been found. However, it is still not exactly the Grail of the classical legend. This paradox actually leads to the first connection that will reveal the true nature of the Grail. Evidence available so far points to two containers, which may or may not have had anything to do with the Last Supper. These two vessels were used to collect Christ's blood and were entombed with the body of Jesus. However, there are still the traditions of the Grail legend in which Joseph and Nicodemus each possess two cruets containing some of Christ's blood. Lastly, there is Olympiodorus's historical reference to the Marian Chalice and the relic of Mary Magdalene's alabaster jar, both containing the blood of Jesus. With so many "Grails," and with good reason for believing each claim, how is it possible to make any sense of them all or to find out anything about the simple truth at the heart of the Grail legend?

The only way to break through the barrier between the true Grail and all of these conflicting, chaotic historical reports is to question everything. Forget all that has been previously learned. Consider that each may have in fact possessed an amount of this blood. Since Joseph, Nicodemus, and Mary were present during the crucifixion and the preparation of Christ's body, they would have been there together to witness any collection of blood that might have occurred, both after the crucifixion and in the tomb. Similarly, after the resurrection, surely any blood left behind in these containers would have seemed sacred, touched almost by the very spirit of God—so sacred that it was deemed necessary to take it and preserve it as an early icon around which Christ's teachings could continue. In essence, each of the three persons could have had a Grail. However, how does one consolidate the Grail tradition, in its classical form, and all of these other Grails? The answer is quite simple. The historical Holy Grail was more than one object.

12

THE NANTEOS CUP

Researching the Grail is researching the true nature of myth itself. By definition, the Grail is something that simultaneously is, and is not, both physical and metaphysical. Therefore, it becomes a game of fact-finding and rethinking that enables the Grail researcher to begin understanding the true nature of the relic as a historical object. If one sets out in search of one thing in particular, it is almost certain that it will never be found. However, if one begins researching the legend with the mindset that wherever the facts and history take the study, that is where the student of Grail lore will find the answers.

It is clear that the Grail legend is much larger, more convoluted, and far more elaborate than the search for the truth behind the legend. In fact the most useful tool in historical research is an open mind—a mind willing to unlearn. Therefore, the path to discovering the true nature of the Grail cup used at the Last Supper is to realize that it may not be that at all. However, along this path, it is also quite likely that a reason for this inherent supposition can be found.

Just as the investigation of the Grail legend cannot exclude Glastonbury, research of the historical authenticity of a modern candidate for the Grail cannot exclude the Nanteos Cup of Wales. Owned by the Powell family, this small, shattered relic is one of the least known among the possible historical Grail candidates. However, its story is worthy of consideration, both for its history and for its claims of health-bringing properties.

The Powell family and the Manor House itself have quite an interesting history: "Although the present building dates only from the 18th

century there has been a house on the site ever since the 11th century"
(*Nanteos Manor Guide Book*, p. 28).

> The present house was built in the 18th century, started in 1739,
> as you will see from the foundation stone on the right of the main
> entrance. This is not, however, the first house on the site. Origi-
> nally there were two houses, one on either side of the valley. In one
> lived the Jones family, and in the other the Powells.
> Thomas Powell, who built the present house, was the son of the
> son of William Powell, who had married the grand-daughter of
> Colonel John Jones of Nanteos. Colonel Jones defended Aberys-
> twyth castle against Cromwell during the Civil war. He had three
> daughters but no son. The second daughter, Anne, married Cor-
> nelius le Brun. Le Brun came from an old Huguenot family which
> had settled in Cologne. He was an engineer, and, presumably came
> to Cardiganshire to work in the silver and lead mines which flour-
> ished locally. He became High Sheriff of the county and acquired
> the Sunnyhill estate at Tregaron. His daughter, Averina le Brun,
> became the wife of William, a son of Thomas Powell, who had
> been one of the judges at the trial of the Seven Bishops, in 1688.
> Thus the two houses were united.
> Thomas, the elder son of William and Averina, became the
> Member of Parliament for Cardiganshire. He married Mary,
> grand-daughter of Sir John Frederick, the Lord Mayor of Lon-
> don, and sister of the Duchess of Atholl. In 1738, William Pow-
> ell died at the age of eighty. Immediately his son began building
> the new house [*Nanteos Manor Guide Book*, p. 30].

According to this guide book, the Powell family owned most of
Aberystwyth, having made their fortune from their other properties
and lead mines in the area.

The story of the Nanteos Cup begins, curiously enough, at the site
agreed to be the focal point for all the Grail legends—Glastonbury.
According to Powell family tradition, the cup came to be in their possession through a series of events tracing it way back to the Grail traditions of Glastonbury. When the abbey risked destruction by Cromwell
under the supervision of King Henry VIII, the last Abbot of Glastonbury, Richard Whiting, commanded a few of his monks to take one of
their most prized relics, a small cup, from the abbey where it had been
hidden in the walls. These monks found their way to the Cistercian
abbey of Strata Florida, where they wished to make a new Glastonbury.
However, advancing danger pushed them further into Wales, to the
site of the Nanteos Manor. As time passed, the olive wood cup was

The Nanteos Cup (by permission of the Rev. Peter Scothern, Nanteos).

protected by these monks who served as the private abbots of the Powell family church.

There the monks found safe refuge for many years, and one by one began to pass away. When the last of the Glastonbury monks reached the end of his days, he entrusted the wooden cup to the Lord of Nanteos Manor and gave him the cryptic commandment to keep it safe, "until the church claims her own." Whether this meant until the church retakes the cup, or until the end of time, we will never know. Even now the graves of the monks who guarded this Grail cup can be found on the grounds of the Nanteos Manor. This cup was kept in hiding to protect the precious relic until 1878, when the owners of Nanteos Manor decided to put the cup on display.

The cup had been kept in a box, covered with a velvet shroud, along with several papers and documents that testify to the long history of miraculous healings that have been associated with the cup. These documents tell of cured arthritis, diseases, even the severe head injury of a young member of the Powell family caused by a riding accident. The bowl exists now as only half of what it once was. The teeth of the devoted pilgrims and not-so-devoted relic hunters have literally eaten away at the wood of the cup until it now consists of only one side and most of the base.

Although the healing effects associated with this bowl might be questioned, such claims of healing due to this relic date back as far as 500 years. The parish priest, Reverend Peter Scothern, still receives hundreds of requests for prayer cloths that have been dipped in the water poured over the remains of the Nanteos Cup. In like manner, letters of thanks for healed illness continue to stream in to the Reverend Scothern. For example,

> A DEAF MAN HEARS—I live in the Godavari District. My hearing was greatly impaired. Through your blessed prayer cloth I heard God's voice. Now I am completely healed [Testimony of L. Kumar as sent to the Rev. Peter Scothern].

The Nanteos Cup has in its long history attracted more than simply the ill, the faithful, or the Grail seeker. Before composing his now famous opera, *Parsifal,* Richard Wagner visited the Nanteos Manor and heard the story of the cup that at the time resided there. Upon seeing the cup, Wagner went to the study where he began making notes for his yet-to-be-composed opera.

As with all the possible contenders for the role of historical Grail, the Nanteos Cup cannot be proven as authentic. Some historians believe this cup to be nothing more than a simple medieval serving dish, made of elm instead of olive wood, found while excavating the manor's foundation. However, its association with Glastonbury does beg further investigation. Furthermore, when one thinks of the Grail as the cup of the Last Supper, one would surely think of a simple wooden bowl such as this. To further understand the Nanteos Cup's place in our modern Grail theory, it is necessary to see if it fits the description of an object, either culinary or funerary, which might have been used as the Grail legend dictates.

Most people familiar with the Grail legend would immediately see the Nanteos Cup as a simple wooden cup that might have been used at the Last Supper—a meal intended to objectify humility and simplicity, led by a man who revered the same qualities. However, archeological and historical data would seem to disagree with such a conclusion, as illustrated by the following description of a cup.

> Although cups were usually made from pottery, some were formed of precious metals, such as gold and silver. They could resemble either modern cups or shallow bowls. People drank from them, but they also had other purposes.

> By New Testament times, glass cups—usually goblet-shaped—
> had been introduced. The cup used for the Last Supper was prob-
> ably a pottery bowl big enough to hold some wine for all present
> [*Illustrated Dictionary of Bible Life and Times*, p. 94].

The Grail as the cup of the Last Supper therefore would not indicate a cup made out of wood, rather one of pottery or possibly of glass.
However, what about another possibility? It is also said that the Grail
could have been a dish used at the Last Supper instead of a cup. What
does archeology say about a dish in the same circumstances? Unfortunately, a dish would have been made from the same materials, except
for one outstanding difference.

> A dish could be a plate, a platter, or a shallow or deep bowl. Most
> dishes were used to hold or serve food and were made of pottery.
> Wooden dishes were highly valued, and those made of gold and
> other precious metals were used in the households of the rich and
> in the sanctuary [*Illustrated Dictionary of Bible Life and Times*,
> p. 107].

Although the Nanteos Cup as a bowl, dish, or cup from the Last
Supper seems unlikely, it is certainly not out of the question. Archeological evidence does point toward another possibility—that of the cup
being used as an object of reverence or of sacred importance. Olive oil
was used to anoint the kings of Israel and as a religious offering. Similarly, wood from the olive tree was seen as nearly sacred—used for
objects of great importance.

> Olive wood was used for fine cabinetwork; the two cherubim guard-
> ing the temple's inner sanctuary were made of olive wood (1 Kings
> 6:23). The olive tree symbolized fertility and peace. The dove
> released by Noah returned with an olive branch, the first sign of
> life after the flood (Gen. 8:11) [*Illustrated Dictionary of Bible Life
> and Times*, p. 255].

It is apparent that the Nanteos Cup as a vessel used for eating,
drinking, or serving food at the Last Supper is rather unlikely. However, it would be more likely that such a container made of olive wood
would be an object of greater importance, such as a container for precious oils, possibly for anointing a person's body, or for use as a religious offering.

The question must now be asked, if the Nanteos Cup is not the cup of the Last Supper, what role, if any, does it play in the Grail legend? Since the cup has been kept in such secrecy by the Powell family, there is little historical reference to this cup in relation to the Grail. The closest link to the legend is in the cup's association to Glastonbury, utilizing the fame of the Joseph of Arimathea legend.

If it were indeed found at Glastonbury, one might think this is the cup Joseph brought to Britain, but this small wooden cup is nothing like the short, round, flaired-lip cruets or vials depicted in any of the illustrations of Joseph's arrival at Britain with the two relics. Furthermore, this is one relic, not two as the Joseph legend dictates. Although these facts would seem to invalidate the Nanteos Cup as the historical Grail, the paradox shall prove to be at the very heart of the final discovery of the Grail's true nature.

It has been determined that there has been at least some confusion regarding the Grail legend and other relics of Christ's Passion. There were allegedly several Holy Lances, several copies or pieces of the True Cross, many different crowns of thorns—in fact, almost every relic carries some amount of confused history in its legend. Therefore, it is not surprising that one would find such mixing and confusion in the Grail legend. However, the key to unraveling this mystery comes again from simple history.

The earliest reliable reference to the Grail is that of Olympiodorus and his reference to the Empress Helena finding a relic referred to as the Marian Chalice along with the other items of the Arma Christi. The question was raised why Helena called this object a chalice, and why it was associated with Mary. Since Mary the mother of Jesus is almost never associated with any relic of the Passion, it is assumed that the reference is made to Mary Magdalene.

The history of this enigmatic relic states that it was sent to Britain for protection during the attacks on Rome. Although some scholars of the Grail legend place the chalice in Roman settlements in Britain at the time, Glastonbury would be a more logical place for the relic to be sent during such times of danger. Therefore, the Marian Chalice, the firmest link between reliable history and the Grail legend, must have been at Glastonbury. This fact may have been the reason why the Arthur legend is so closely tied to the Grail. Therefore, a cup such as this found at Glastonbury would reasonably be considered as the Marian Chalice.

Considering that the Marian Chalice most likely would have been sent to Glastonbury, a center for the protection of blood relics as reflected by the Joseph legend, the Nanteos Cup fits the description of the chalice very closely. The cup was found hidden in the walls of Glastonbury and is made of olive wood—a material considered quite valuable and nearly sacred in Palestine during the time of Christ.

The question remains, however, why was this cup associated with Mary Magdalene instead of Joseph of Arimathea? To answer this question, the confused history of relics must again be considered. The Joseph legend says that he came to Britain with two vials containing the sweat and blood of Christ. These containers are portrayed in stained glass windows and other images as two small objects that resemble jars with small lids or covers. Both objects would be small enough to fit into one hand. The Nanteos Cup obviously does not fit this description. It does, however, fit the description of what normally would be called a cup or chalice. Since this cup was found hidden at Glastonbury, where the Marian Chalice was most likely sent, it is probably not the original relic brought to Britain by Joseph. It is more likely a separate relic, the Marian Chalice itself, sent to Britain in AD 410, specifically due to the preexisting history of Joseph bringing blood relics to Glastonbury in the form of the two cruets or vials of blood and sweat.

Illustration taken from a detail of a stained glass window in the Church of Saint John near Glastonbury, showing Joseph of Arimathea holding the cruets that were originally associated with the Grail (Keith Ellis).

Why the Nanteos Cup is referred to as the Marian Chalice is still a bit of a mystery. The most that can be done is a bit of historical detective work—circumstantial evidence leading to a most probable answer. It has been said that there might have been a preexisting notion of a container, related to Mary Magdalene, that once contained the blood of Christ. This notion may have been what caused Empress Helena to call the vessel she found in the tomb the Marian Chalice. This idea seems quite likely if one reviews both Hebrew funerary practice and the account of the crucifixion as seen in the Bible.

The custom of Hebrew burial was to take the body to an upper room, or living space, of a family member and anoint it with oils and perfumes as an act of honoring their beloved dead. This practice was coupled with another important custom—collecting any blood that spilled from the corpse. However, this practice could not be performed as it normally would have been with Christ's body. All burial rituals had to be accelerated due to the Sabbath that was rapidly approaching. Therefore, instead of taking Christ's body to an upper room, it was taken directly to the tomb. However, the practice of collecting the blood still would have been conducted.

Either in the hope that they could conduct the ceremony as planned or simply in doing the best they could under the circumstances, some-one would have gone to the upper room that Christ's followers intended to use for His preparations, most likely the room of the Last Supper. While there, the person sent to the upper room would have gathered the things necessary for the ritual, including a cup to hold the spilled blood. When it became apparent that the body could not be taken to the upper room, the person sent there would have taken as much of the items collected for this purpose as were still needed. This is the most likely explanation for the idea of the Holy Grail being the cup used at the Last Supper—it came from the same upper room.

By the time this person arrived, Joseph probably would have been taking Christ down from the cross, allowing even more blood to be spilled on the ground. Here one must consider that Mary Magdalene would have been one of the Marys said to have been at the foot of the cross in the Bible. Since Joseph intended to use his own burial items for Christ, including the agate cup atop the Santo Cáliz, there would have been two cups present at the crucifixion that could be used to collect the blood.

Since the cup brought from the upper room would have been more common, made of ceramic or wood, it would have been used to collect the blood spilled on the ground, while Joseph's agate cup would have been saved for use in the tomb. Joseph took Jesus down from the cross, and Nicodemus helped him. Therefore one must ask, who collected the blood? This would leave only the three Marys available to perform this task. It is likely that Mary Magdalene used the cup taken from the room of the Last Supper to collect the bloodied dirt at the foot of the cross and any that fell to the ground while the body was being taken to

Joseph's tomb. If this cup was left in the tomb for Helena to find centuries later, it rightly could be called the Marian Chalice since Mary
Magdalene had used it to collect Christ's blood.

It seems clear that the small, wooden cup known as the Nanteos
Cup, worn and chipped away by the devoted, is in fact the same object
as the Marian Chalice. Found by Empress Helena upon her discovery
of Christ's tomb in Jerusalem, this chalice was kept for many years as
a holy relic, among many others found in the tomb. When danger
threatened what Helena saw as the Grail, she elected to send it to Britain
where it could be safely guarded. However, it was not sent to a fortress
where it could again be put in harm's way, rather to a place of great sanctity and holy worth. At Glastonbury, the Marian Chalice found a safe
refuge, housed with whatever relics were taken to Britain by Joseph of
Arimathea.

There it rested, possibly lost, rediscovered, moved, and hidden over
the centuries, until political pressures again threatened the relic's existence. Then it was moved from Glastonbury to another secret hiding
place in Strata Florida. In the hands of the expatriated monks of Glastonbury, the cup came to rest on the grounds of what would one day
become Nanteos Manor. Finally, the Marian Chalice, now known as
the Nanteos Cup, would find safety after a tumultuous journey throughout time and across the breadth of Christendom.

This cup may in fact be the one thread that would stitch together
the scattered aspects of the Grail legend to include the Last Supper,
Joseph of Arimathea, and King Arthur into one congruent legend of
which most are now familiar. However, in the search for the Holy Grail
of history, this is simply one face of the True Grail. There still remains
one part of the Grail legend, the tradition of Joseph bringing two vials
to Britain, that must be fully understood. The same open mind that
allowed an understanding of the Nanteos Cup will in fact lead to the
unexpected truth at the heart of the Grail legend.

13

PERSONAL RELIQUARIES

The undisputed father of the Grail legend is Joseph of Arimathea, the man who brought two cruets of Christ's blood and sweat to Britain. Glastonbury and its famous abbey were founded by Joseph before AD 100. However, the only alleged Grail cup found at Glastonbury was later translated to Nanteos Manor in Wales, and it was not the two cruets associated with Joseph. It was a small olive wood cup which would seem to be the Marian Chalice of Olympiodorus's histories. Also, this cup was not brought to Britain by Joseph, but was discovered by Empress Helena and sent to Britain in AD 410.

This presents an interesting paradox for the Grail researcher. The Grail legend has always hinged on Joseph's role as the keeper of this sacred relic. However, the best evidence available for a historical Grail is centered on the Nanteos Cup that appears to have nothing to do with Joseph. One may think that the Grail legend in its traditional form may have been a corruption of a different tradition in which the cruets depicted with Joseph were actually this wooden cup. However, there are several problems with this assumption. Joseph was considered to be the keeper of the Grail long before AD 410. Also, if the Nanteos Cup is the Marian Chalice, it would have been sent to Glastonbury due to the pre-existing history of Glastonbury as a center for the keeping of Christ's blood relics. This would mean that Joseph did indeed bring two vials of blood there three centuries before just as tradition indicates.

The problem is that if Joseph did bring his Grails to Britain, and the Nanteos Cup is also the Grail found in Christ's tomb, how did there

come to be two Grails instead of the one and only Grail that the legend speaks of? The question is contradictory. The legend as we have it
today is in truth only one face of many placed on the Grail. An investigation of the Grail romances renders a Grail that has been seen as a
number of things, sometimes even several things within the same text.
Other than being resplendent in its rich, golden beauty, the Grail is first
described simply as "graal" by Chrétien. His continuators later added
further detail, saying that it gave food in plenty to all the knights who
sat around the Rich Fisher King's banquet table. The relic is first
described as "The Holy Grail" in Robert de Boron's *Joseph d'Arimathie*.
After this, the Grail becomes some type of alchemical talisman in Wolfram's *Parzifal*.

It is clear to see that the Grail has only recently been considered
as one relic. Amid this sea of Grails, there is an answer, albeit largely
overlooked, that can clarify these contradictory themes. In fact, the con-
tradiction between Joseph's vials and the Nanteos Cup is provided by
the Grail texts themselves. The First Continuation of Chrétien's Grail
romance makes an intriguing statement of which most are unaware. It
claims that, in addition to the Grail that provides food to the warriors
at the Fisher King's table, there is a second Grail that can be found in
Lucca, Italy. This Grail is not the golden cup of which Chrétien spoke,
or in fact a cup at all. It is a carving of Christ, made by Nicodemus as
an act of reverence after witnessing the crucifixion. This reference might
be passed off as an interesting bit of fancy inserted into the Grail legend if it were not for the simple fact that there is indeed a carving of
Christ, allegedly fashioned by Nicodemus, in the town of Lucca, Italy.

Called the Volto Santo, this carving was found to contain two
blood relics hidden around the base of the skull or the neck. This link
between the Grail texts and history is remarkable, to say the least. However, it is more remarkable that this is not the only vial or set of vials
that can be found around Europe that claim to be the Grail.

The Volto Santo

Saint Martin's Cathedral in Lucca, Italy, is home to one of the most
unusual relics which has been named as the Holy Grail. This sacred
object is not a cup, a bowl, or a dish. It is instead a face—a Holy Face.
The Volto Santo of Lucca is a carving of Jesus as He hangs crucified on
a large, dark cross. Written around AD 1190, the First Continuation of

Drawing of the Volto Santo (reproduced from a photograph) (Keith Ellis).

The Cathedral of Saint Martin in Lucca, Italy (Claudia Lüdtke).

Chrétien's story of Perceval describes two Grails. While the first Grail is said to be a chalice, made for Joseph to collect Christ's blood at the crucifixion, the second Grail is the Volto Santo, which is specifically said to be found in Lucca.

Although the tale told here says that Nicodemus, the maker of this carving, only fashioned the likeness of Christ's face and head, the Volto

The Chapel of the Volto Santo (Claudia Lüdtke).

Santo is a wooden representation of Jesus on the cross, head slightly tilted down and to the right, wearing a blue tunic. The story of the Volto Santo is that Nicodemus left it to Isaachar, or Isaac, before he died in Palestine. Isaac kept it in his house for private worship during the years of the early church. There it remained, its guardianship passed down throughout the generations, until it was sent to Italy during the Iconoclastic Period. It arrived at the Magra River near Luni in 742 and, upon inspection, was found to contain two small vials of blood hidden in the neck.

Although the two cruets found inside the head were split between the bishops of Luni and Lucca, what is important is that we see the repeating pattern of blood-filled vials continued here with the Volto Santo, an object created by Nicodemus apparently to contain Jesus' blood relics. Furthermore, we see this particular relic mentioned in one of our Grail texts, the First Continuation, the first text to indicate the Christian significance of the Grail.

It is quite interesting to hear of another follower of Jesus, other than Joseph, having two vials of blood held as relics of the crucifixion. It would appear that the tradition of Joseph and his two cruets is simply part of a much larger family of relics that may be the true Holy Grail. Are there any other vials about which such a claim can be made? There turn out to be many more than one might think.

Victoria Palmer's Onyx Cup

Next in line among the most likely Grail candidates is a small vial found in Shropshire, England. Graham Phillips introduced the Hawstone Park cup to the field of Grail research in his 1995 book, *The Search for the Grail*. He brings to light the first, best historical reference for the physical existance of the Grail by referencing the fifth century Greek historian, Olympiodorus. In his *Materials for History*, variously called the "22 Fragments of Olympiodorus," he writes of the Empress Helena Augusta discovering the Marian Chalice in Christ's tomb, then how the cup was later sent to Britain for safety in AD 410 during the attacks on Rome.

Phillips outlines the historical evidence for the historical King Arthur being the Celtic ruler Owain Ddantgwyn, and how his kingdom was actually Virconium, the last, greatest Roman city in Britain, which is now the Shropshire region of Western Britain. He continues

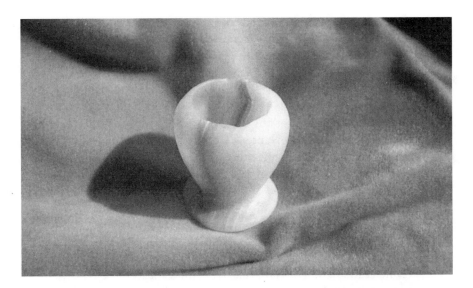

The Hawstone Park Vial, one of the possible unguent flasks owned by Mary Magdalene and used as a reliquary to hold small amounts of Christ's blood (*The Search for the Grail* by Graham Phillips).

to offer substantial literary and historical evidence suggesting that the Marian Chalice arrived in Virconium from Rome since the city was seen as the best Roman fortification to protect this sacred relic. Once he establishes this point, he demonstrates how the cup has been handed down, lost, and rediscovered by the descendants of Owain, until it finally found refuge in a grotto in Hawstone Park, hidden away in the base of a statue.

While the literary trail that led him to the account of the cup's discovery in the grotto is very clearly important, his assessment of the cup's history is hinged on his theory regarding the historical King Arthur and the location of his seat of power. The evidence which supports his conclusions regarding Owain Ddantgwyn at Virconium has been questioned in the British archeological world and is still less accepted than the site at Cadbury. Regardless of who is the historical King Arthur or the site of his Camelot, it would be more likely that the Marian Chalice, the cup found in the tomb of Christ, would be sent to Britain for one reason only.

Glastonbury in Britain has long been considered the most sacred ground on the British Isles. The reason behind this notion was the legend of Joseph of Arimathea and his arrival at Glastonbury with the two cruets containing the holy blood of Jesus. From the first century AD, Glastonbury has been a center for Christian devotion and reverence. Considering this, it would be much more likely that a sacred relic such as the Marian Chalice would be sent to Britain, not to a fortified Roman city, but to Glastonbury—home for other relics of Christ's Passion for the previous 300 years.

Keeping in mind that the Marian Chalice was probably sent to Glastonbury, making the Nanteos Cup the most likely candidate for being the Marian Chalice, one must question the idea of this tiny onyx vial being the Grail cup found by Helena in Christ's tomb. The Nanteos Cup was not only found at Glastonbury, but it is more likely that this would be called a chalice by Helena than the tiny onyx vial found in Hawstone Park. However, one cannot lightly brush off this discovery. The trail left behind outlining the path to its resting place is much too old and obviously important for this object to be a simple hoax.

The Hawstone Park vial is clearly significant to the Grail legend. It may not be the Marian Chalice from Christ's tomb, but it does bear a striking resemblance to the description of one of the cruets belonging to Joseph of Arimathea. It is short, and round, with a small pedestal base. There appears to have been a flared lip on top at one point, probably capped by a small lid making it a closed container, just as the Joseph legend states.

Why then is it not included with the relics of Glastonbury in Nanteos? One must consider that Glastonbury is said to have contained many relics, both of saints and of Christ's Passion. The Nanteos Cup is only one of these. Therefore, these relics must have been scattered, or distributed, as protection against their being lost through time and man's folly. This notion is perfectly illustrated by the following passage taken from the last chapter of *Perlesvaus*, speaking of Perceval and the others of his family who served as guardians of the Grail and its related relics.

> Therein abode they even as it pleased God, until that his mother passed away and his sister and all they that were therein save he alone. The hermits that were nigh the castle buried them and sang their masses, and came every day and took counsel of him for the holiness they saw him do and the good life that he led there. So one day whilst he was in the holy chapel where the hallows were, forthwith, behold you, a Voice that cometh down therein: "Perceval," saith the Voice, "Not long shall you abide herein; wherefore it is God's will that you dispart the hallows amongst the hermits

of the forest, there where these bodies shall be served and worshipped, and the most Holy Graal shall appear herein no more,but
within a brief space shall you know well the place where it shall
be."

If the Grail Hallows were scattered across the land, the vial found
at Hawstone Park is likely one of the two cruets brought to Britain by
Joseph of Arimathea, and it could also be called a Grail. This is just
one of the vials, however. What might have happened to the second?
The answer to this question can be found in Rome where another vial
is claimed to be the true Grail.

Rocco Zingaro's Italian Templar Vial

An article entitled "The Holy Grail Is Found" printed in the
August 18, 1995, edition of the *Boston Globe* makes the statement that
the true Grail appears to be in Italy, not Hawstone Park in England.
Rocco Zingaro di San Ferdinando, the Grand Master of the Italian
order of the Knights Templar, claims that they are in possession of a
green glass flask which is the true Holy Grail.

Zingaro says that he obtained the Grail 20 years before from Anto-
nio Ambrosini, a late Italian academic and former member of their
order. He states that Ambrosini found the Grail in a Coptic monastary
in Egypt and gave it to Zingaro as a wedding gift.

Although the article states that Zingaro was simply one of many
who had claimed to possess the true Grail, the validity of his claim is
not altogether unlikely. The vial Zingaro is shown holding can be
described as being approximately two to three inches tall with a flattened
base, a bulbous body, and a narrow neck topped with a flattened, flared
lip.

In most of the illustrations and other depictions of Joseph of Arimathea with his flasks, he is seen holding two short containers with a
rounded body and a flaired lip. The vial held by Rocco Zingaro matches
the description quite well. Another interesting fact of Zingaro's vial is
that, although it is made of a different material, it looks almost iden-
tical to the vial found in Hawstone Park. The English vial is made of
onyx, but it has almost the exact same shape as the Italian vial, with
the exception of its English counterpart's flared lip that has been

broken off. If this is Joseph's other cruet, it is very likely that, during the scattering of the relics, this vial was sent to another chapel on the isle of Britain that once held relics.

Rosslyn Chapel in Scotland was built by the St. Clair family, the remainders of the once-great Knights Templar. This magnificent chapel, decorated literally from floor to ceiling with images of worship, is said to have once held a portion of the True Cross. Although Rosslyn legend says that the Holy Grail is hidden inside the Apprentice Pillar in the sanctuary, there is another link to the Grail legend that is much more likely.

Since Rocco Zingaro claims to be the modern-day heir to the glory of his ancient brotherhood, the Knights Templar, this vial relic might be the lost cruet of Joseph, sent to Rosslyn for safety, and later taken to Rome to be protected by the Knights Templar through the ages. Although there is little evidence to support Zingaro's claim, looking at his glass vial next to the onyx vial found in Hawstone Park illuminates a similarity which is difficult to dismiss. Since this glass cruet is claimed to be the Holy Grail by the modern Roman Templars, it is quite likely that this is the Grail in the sense that, like the Hawstone Park vial, Joseph carried it from Palestine to Britain.

Mary Magdalene and the Alabaster Jar

Along with the cruets or vials owned by Joseph of Arimathea and Nicodemus, there is one more vial that is associated with another individual mentioned in the story of Christ's entombment—Mary Magdalene. When her body was discovered in France, an object described as an alabaster flask was also discovered entombed with her. Although little is known about this flask, it is said to have contained a small amount of blood. This was the only flask found with the body—much different than the two belonging to Joseph and Nicodemus. However, it does fit in with the notion of the Grail as a small container holding blood relics from the crucifixion. Although the relic is no longer on display, it supposedly still resides near the tomb of Mary Magdalene in Sainte Maximin, France.

Along with the Nanteos Cup and Santo Cáliz of Valencia, there now appear to be a number of new Grails to add to the list. If Joseph's cruets, the two originally brought to Britain, are to be considered as

Grails, then also are those of Nicodemus and Mary Magdalene. That means that today one can find such vials in Hawstone Park, England; possibly Rome, Italy; Lucca, Italy; and Sainte Maximin, France. These items could be considered as personal reliquaries, obtained by the three people who were present during the preparation of Christ's body for entombment.

If all these objects should be considered to be the Grail, what role did they play? How did they become part of the Grail legend? Should they be part of the historical truth of the Grail at all? The Grail began as one mysterious, elusive object, with a nearly impossible history to reconstruct, and now it seems to have become many different things. The search for the true Grail has returned to the state in which it began—a confusion of too many histories and claims to validity. How can any answers be gathered from all this? As with any puzzle, the most difficult task lies in getting past the mass of jumbled pieces, and understanding how they all fit together.

14

MARY MAGDALENE AND THE ALABASTRON

When investigating a historical mystery, without exception the most difficult aspect is learning more about the principal characters of the story. To fully understand a historical event, the people who made the history must be as fully understood as possible. There is the difficulty. To know about the character and history of a person who has been dead for one or two thousand years is a feat in itself. The principal characters of the Grail story are those who were present at Christ's crucifixion—Joseph of Arimathea, Nicodemus, and, of course Mary Magdalene.

A modern study of the Grail legend would be incomplete without a discussion of Mary Magdalene. Although there were about three women mentioned by the name Mary in the New Testament, many biblical scholars agree that the Mary who participated in the crucifixion and in the interment of Jesus's body was Mary Magdalene. She was the woman who broke open the alabaster box of spikenard and anointed His feet and/or head with the costly, perfumed oil. She was the woman who brought more oils for Christ's body after it had been hurriedly entombed just before the Sabbath.

It has been demonstrated that Mary, after she opened the box of nard and used it to anoint Jesus, would have felt the need to complete the task when the time actually came to place Christ in Joseph's new tomb. However, little has been said about the custom, the materials used, or the meaning behind this act of reverence. Although Mary felt a compulsion to perform this act properly during the entombment process, what might have led her to do this initially? This is where the investigation into the character of Mary Magdalene must begin.

In recent years, Mary has found a place of reverence in the field of Grail research. However, her place in legend has been debated almost since the time of Christ. She has been associated with several other mysteries such as the Black Madonnas found troughout Europe, icons of the Virgin Mary which do not fit with the rules of conventional iconography, the Priory of Sion and the Rennes le Château mystery. Recent theories state that she not only played an important role in the Grail legend, but was herself the founder of the Grail, but in a most unexpected way.

This theory was reported in the 1983 book, *Holy Blood, Holy Grail*, by Michael Baigent, Richard Leigh, and Henry Lincoln. Their theory in summary states that Mary Magdalene was the mother to several children fathered by Jesus. They claim that these children were sired either just before the crucifixion or in a long marriage afterwards, resulting in the obvious conclusion that the entire crucifixion was a hoax and never took place as described. Although this theory has found a nearly zealous popularity among its readers, there have been several concerns expressed about its validity.

Although there appears to be no written account of Christ's crucifixion outside of the Bible, the event is accepted as an actual historical event. The death of Jesus on the cross would, however, appear to stand up to a trail of circumstantial evidence, which is what most history and archeology of the time is built upon. Although it is ultimately not possible to verify the historical validity of this event beyond question, the problems inherent in the Holy Blood theory do not rest on this one point alone.

In the latter half of their book about the Holy Blood theory, they state that they noticed the repeating theme of the Grail in their historical research. For example, Godfroi de Bouillon was, according to medieval legend, descended from Lohengrin, the Knight of the Swan, who was in one Grail text the son of Perceval, the original Grail hero. However, the real similarities seem to arise when comparing several aspects of the Arthur legend to the Merovingian Empire.

As a result of this distinctly British emphasis, we had not automatically associated the Grail with the Merovingian dynasty. And yet Wolfram insists that Arthur's court is at Nantes and that his poem is set in France. The same assertion is made by other Grail romances—the *Queste del Saint Graal*, for instance. And there are medieval traditions that maintain the Grail was not brought to Britain by Joseph of Arimathea, but to France by the Magdalen.

We now began to wonder whether the preeminence assigned to Britain by commentators on the Grail romances had not perhaps been misplaced and whether the romances in fact referred primarily to events on the continent—more particularly to events in France. And we began to suspect that the Grail itself, the "blood royal," actually referred to the blood royal of the Merovingian dynasty—a blood that was deemed to be sacred and invested with magical or miraculous properties [Baigent, Leigh, and Lincoln, p. 307–308].

This assertion, both that Arthur's court was in France, and that the writers of the original Grail texts were mistaken or somehow unfamiliar with the histories and traditions of their own country, seems unlikely at best. There is little if any evidence of Arthur being in France, much less his fabled Camelot. Further, the court of Marie of Champagne was known to be a center for learning and knowledge at the time. It is very unlikely that Chrétien de Troyes would have missed the opportunity to place King Arthur in the land of his patron court, had there been any evidence to support it.

The association of King Arthur with the Merovingians shadows by comparison, however, to the claim that this empire sprang from a union between Jesus and Mary Magdalene. The claim that Baigent, Leigh, and Lincoln put forth is that Mary's actions seem to indicate a role of wife to Jesus, thus leading to the thought that they must have been married and had children.

For this to be true, one of three things must have happened. First, Mary and Jesus must have known each other for some time before they were said to have met at the house of Mary's sister, Martha. There is no evidence of this in the Bible. The greatest amount of time any of the Gospels puts between the Last Supper and their meeting is six days. However, due to the translation conventions implemented in converting the original Gospels from Greek to Latin, this may have been derived from a statement that actually meant, "In the six days before (the Passover.") Other accounts of this meeting place it only two days before the Passover feast. Second, Jesus and Mary must have had a sexual encounter just before the crucifixion. Considering the Bible's account of the things Jesus did during that time, this would have been nearly a logistical impossibility. It is also unlikely, because even if such a union would have taken place, and if Mary became pregnant, she would have had only one or two children, not the "family" that the Holy Blood theory would seem to indicate. Third, Jesus would have lived after the crucifixion. This would require that either the entire crucifixion narrative was a hoax, or that Jesus somehow survived being hung from a cross and a spear thrust through His side.

This third possibility is mostly what the authors of the *Holy Blood, Holy Grail* use to perpetuate the theory. However, there are several glaring problems with this approach. The most obvious problem would be with the faking of Christ's crucifixion. To completely fabricate such an event would involve an almost global conspiracy involving people down through time. This theory claims the crucifixion was a hoax largely because there appeared to be no good reason to crucify Jesus. However, the most cursory investigation into the practice of crucifixion would destroy this idea. Jesus taught a doctrine taking ultimate power and homage away from the Roman Emperor and giving it to God. To the Roman magistrate, this would be seen as treason, tantamount to the modern-day trading of defense secrets.

Furthermore, the idea that early Christians would want to hide any survivors of Christ, or that Christ himself survived, is against both common sense and basic human psychology. Christ's followers were in a state of chaos following His death, literally wondering where to turn. If Jesus Himself, or one of His descendants, still survived, they would have immediately made him the new Messiah—the new leader of their burgeoning Christian church. Looking at the nature of this early Christian church, one finds another fact that would indicate a breakup of their leadership. After Christ's death, His followers dispersed for the most part, going their separate ways across Europe. If there had been one central leader among them, they would have remained in a group as they had been.

The historical proof used to justify the Holy Blood theory is exemplified by the following passage where Jesus has come to raise Lazarus from the dead. When Mary's sister Martha rushes forth from their house to meet Jesus, Mary remains in the house for a time.

> It would be plausible enough for Mary to be sitting in the house when Jesus arrives in Bethany. In accordance with Jewish custom she would be "sitting shivah"—sitting in mourning. But why does she not join Martha and rush to meet Jesus on his return? There

is one obvious explanantion. By the tenets of Judaic law at the time, a woman "sitting shivah" would have been strictly forbidden to emerge from the house except at the express bidding of her husband. In this incident the behavior of Jesus and Mary of Bethany conforms precisely to the traditional comportment of a Jewish husband and wife [Baigent, Leigh, and Lincoln, p. 336].

To those who subscribe to this theory, this and other examples of this nature would indicate that Mary Magdalene was married to Jesus. However, the simplest knowledge of the Bible would render this argument utterly baseless. Although the authors' facts regarding Hebrew tradition are correct, their reasoning is false. Consider the passage of Jesus asking two fishermen to turn away from their life of fishing and join Him: "Now as he walked by the sea of Galilee he saw Simon and Andrew his brother casting a net into the sea: for they were fishers. And Jesus said unto them, Come ye after me, and I will make you to become fishers of men. And straightway they forsook their nets, and followed him" (The Holy Bible, Mark 1:16–18).

Is one to believe, by the same logic, that here Jesus is married to both Simon and Andrew? Throughout the New Testament, people simply do as Jesus commands. This claim that Mary was Jesus's wife is jumping to a preconceived conclusion using only the most tenuous historical references with which to support it. Granted, this is only one example, but it is much the same as the other examples of proof given in this theory. The authors of *Holy Blood, Holy Grail* themselves admit that to support their theory, they needed to "read between the lines, fill in certain gaps," as well as "look for evidence of circumstances that might have been conducive to a marriage" (p. 330).

One may wonder how this theory came into being. The idea that the Grail is actually a bloodline is derived by a corruption of the word once used to name the Grail—*Sangreal*. This word is customarily split so that it reads *San Greal*, meaning Holy Grail, but the bloodline theory originates from another reading of this word—*Sang Real*, meaning Royal Blood. Before the Holy Blood theory, this was thought to mean the blood of Christ itself since Jesus was both the King of the Jews and descended from King David. However the word *Royal* lead to the thought that the blood of Jesus was not royal by His claims to be King, but royal by way of His offspring who later became the rulers of European empires.

Despite the doubtful claims of the Holy Blood theorists, their conclusions do raise an interesting point. It is clear that Mary Magdalene played a vital role in the creation of the Grail legend. She is present during the crucifixion, she later returns to the tomb with oils to complete Christ's burial ritual, the only reliable historical reference to a Grail-like vessel refers to it as the Marian Chalice, and most importantly, Mary's body was found at Sainte Maximin in France entombed with an alabaster flask containing a small portion of a blood relic. Her task of anointing Jesus when He was in her house in the days before the Last Supper, as well as the alabaster flask with which she was buried, lead to another, more probable interpretation of *Sang Real.*

John Koopmans, who contributed much to this book, draws an important parallel between Mary's alabaster container and the alabaster container that held the pound of the perfumed oil spikenard that Mary used in Christ's anointing. It was a custom during that time for women, both married and unmarried, to wear a small flask of such a perfumed oil around their neck. Although these unguent flasks were called *alabastrons,* they were not necessarily made from alabaster alone. In fact, these ranged from flasks crafted from semiprecious materials such as alabaster, to clay pottery, even including Roman glass. In fact, archeologists have found great quantities of these mass-produced Roman glass unguentaria.

> The rhythm of blow/shear, blow/shear, ... must have made this work remarkably monotonous. Such rapidity of production was the key, however, to why the Roman glassworking industry now embraced free-blowing as its core technology. As the range and quality of free-blown products increased, the demise of glass-casting was swift: its only significant usage after the middle of the 1st century AD was in the production of fine, colorless tablewares. Within the space of just the four decades or so that enfolded the reign of Augustus, glassworking had undergone what can only be described as an industrial revolution, and glass had truly "arrived" as a practical alternative to pottery in many parts of Rome's huge domestic marketplace [Fleming, p. 24].

Grail flasks and urguentaria. *From left to right:* Hawstone Park vial, Rocco Zingaro's vial, an alabastron, a Roman glass unguent vial (1st century AD) (the author).

These alabastrons were used in abundance during the time of Christ and were seen as truly valuable possessions, as judged by Judas's reaction to Mary using one to anoint Jesus. Reviewing the account of this act, it is said that Mary breaks open a box of spikenard containing one pound of the oil. This indeed seems contrary to the use of the alabastron as described above. However, when this passage speaks of Mary breaking the box, it does not mean that the entire box was full of the costly oil. It simply means that she broke the seal that kept this box closed, demonstrating that it was an untouched treasure.

The amount of oil used also indicates a slight misconception. These containers, about the size of a laboratory test tube, would not have contained a pound of the oil. It would have held at best a couple of ounces. Therefore, the box that Mary broke open was most likely a container that held some number of these smaller unguentaria or alabastrons that contained the actual oil.

This fact actually serves to answer one of the greatest questions regarding the other two characters seen at Christ's crucifixion and their role in the Grail legend. Returning to Joseph of Arimathea and Nicodemus, it must be remembered that they too had in their possession vials of this sort. The Volto Santo, carved by Nicodemus, contained two hidden vials of blood relics, and Joseph is said to have arrived at Britain with two cruets (vials) of Christ's blood and sweat. Furthermore, two of the vessels which have been associated with the Grail in recent years, the onyx vial found in Hawstone Park in Shropshire and the glass vial held by the modern-day Templar Rocco Zingaro, bear a very close resemblance to each other. This would lead one to believe that they came from the same source or were fabricated in the same region, even though they are not made of the same material.

In researching ancient Hebrew measures, one may find that what was called a pound is actually about three-quarters of a modern pound. Therefore, if the alabaster box broken open by Mary contained these smaller alabastrons, which probably would have been made of several different materials, and each alabastron contained two ounces each, then there would have been six alabastrons in all—six vials containing 2 ounces each would have totaled 12 ounces, thus fitting the measure of a Hebrew pound.

This would also explain why Joseph and Nicodemus both had two vials holding blood relics and Mary was found to have only one. When Mary broke the box open, she used one to anoint Jesus while He sat at a meal with her and her sister Martha. This would leave only five containers in the box. One would assume this to be the same oil that Mary brought with her to the tomb on the day it was found open (The Holy Bible, Luke 24:1–12). Since Mary was told by Jesus Himself that the oil she used was the first that would prepare His body for burial, the remainder would have been taken to the tomb when she returned to complete the ritual anointing of the deceased's body.

The importance of these five remaining alabastron vials will be seen in the last chapter of this book. These remaining five vials would soon fall into the hands of Joseph and Nicodemus to become the vials with which they have been associated. In the end, it appears that the idea of the *Sang Real*, the Royal Blood, may be valid after all. However, this blood did not come down through time in the veins of the Merovingians or any other dynasty. It came to everyone in modern times in the form of legend, created by the loving acts of Joseph, Nicodemus, and Mary Magdalene.

15

WHAT IS THE GRAIL?

The most haunting aspect of the Grail legend is the ever-present question, hovering just out of reach—what is the Grail? It is both the question the Grail hero must ask and the answer he must find. It is indeed the symbol for man's concept of unattainable perfection, but is it just a simple moral fable? The Grail question may be the conclusion of the Quest, but it also begs an answer. One cannot simply be content in the knowledge that the answer was close. If the answer is just out of reach, one must leap forward, into the abyss, and grasp it.

Many facts have presented themselves along the Grail path, but rather than coming together to form a contiguous whole, they seem to have only made a larger, more perplexing puzzle. Although it appears there are simply a few scattered puzzle pieces along with a great deal of missing information, the truth is that everything necessary to understand the true nature of the Grail has already been seen. From all the information presented in the previous chapters, it is finally possible to understand the truth that lies at the heart of the legend. Not only was the Grail a physical, historical artifact of Christ's life, but the Grail as our culture understands it now is no less than seven different objects.

This theory sounds quite different than the image of the Grail with which most are familiar. However, there are too many differences, discrepancies, and facts that stand out like beacons, all pointing toward a conclusion much different than that of the single Grail cup from the Last Supper. It is the very confusion inherent in the Grail Quest that leads to this conclusion. Everything, including confusion, has its cause, and for each cause, there is a unique set of implications.

The first characteristic that draws one's attention to these incongruities is the diametrically opposed roles attributed to the Grail—the wine cup used by Christ at the Last Supper, and the vessel used to collect His blood at the foot of the cross. The collection of blood at the crucifixion would have taken place as described. However, one must consider the Hebrew custom more carefully to fully understand what took place at the crucifixion.

The funerary rites involved in a Hebrew burial were quite ritualistic. Every drop of blood was collected to be entombed with the body. This would have included any blood that issued from Christ's body either on the cross or in the tomb during preparation. Any other objects with His blood on them would also be included in the tomb, hence the spear, the Crown of Thorns, the nails, etc., as found in the tomb by Helena. Therefore, it is unlikely that a meal plate or drinking vessel used at the Last Supper, or any other meal, would have been used for the collection of blood.

Besides this enigma, there are a host of other conflicts in the traditional Grail saga. Joseph is said to have come to Britain with two cruets of Christ's blood and sweat, instead of a single cup. Several Grail texts claim there is more than one Grail. One such secondary Grail is specifically named as the Volto Santo of Lucca that was carved by Nicodemus. The only historical reference to the Grail is written by Olympiodorus who states a Marian Chalice was found by Helena and sent to Britain in AD 410. To fill these historical roles, there is a list of objects worldwide, each of which claims to be the one and only Grail.

If any sense is to be made of all these incongruent facts, it is necessary to begin finding consistencies and common threads throughout. For example, there is the common theme of people who were close to Christ's body during entombment who possessed vials of His blood. One must now look to the facts for answers. Among the potential historical Grails there are five such vials—two found in the Volto Santo upon its arrival at Luni, the onyx vial found in Hawstone Park, the green glass vial belonging to the Grand Master of the Italian Order of Knights Templar, and finally the alabaster vial found entombed with Mary Magdalene in France. Therefore, it is likely that these vials are, or were based on, the vials used by Joseph, Nicodemus, and Mary to keep a small portion of Jesus' blood as personal relics.

Now that all of the modern candidates for the true historical Holy Grail have been investigated, it is necessary to begin putting the pieces together. Although it is impossible to determine with complete certainty the events of the past, the places, histories, and relics outlined previously can build a probable series of events leading to the formation of the Grail legend. The following is a reconstruction of the events that best answer all questions and accounts for all the archeological evidence present at this time.

The Passage of the True Grail

The events that would eventually become the legend of the Holy Grail begin with Christ's entry into the city of Jerusalem. This began a week of great turmoil, reverence, fear, and devotion. In the days to follow, Jesus found himself at the home of Martha and her sister Mary Magdalene as described previously. Mary, in an act of utmost respect, bathed Christ's feet in a costly oil and was chided by Judas for an act he saw as wasteful. In answer to his protests, Jesus Himself made the statement that this act was done in preparation for His funeral. We may safely assume that Mary then joined the group of Christ's followers, if she and Martha were not part of this group already.

Then came the Passover with Christ's followers. Oddly, this is the one event present in the popular Grail legend that had the least to do with the historical Grail. The synthesis of the Grail was centered mostly on its funerary role—the collection of blood from Christ's body. If a cup from the Last Supper entered the stream of the Grail legend, it was simply in the form of a cup used as a funerary item taken from the same room as that in which the Last Supper was held. The cup from the upper room was taken to the site of the crucifixion where Mary Magdalene used it to collect the blood that spilled onto the earth from Christ's wounds. This is most likely where the idea of the Grail coming from the Last Supper originated.

Someone who went to the room of the Last Supper would have been faced with a great challenge—to find a proper vessel for holding the blood of Christ. Since the Last Supper was a meal glorifying humility and simplicity, it goes without saying that there would have been no gold or silver implements to choose from. This would leave one type of vessel that would have fit the bill—a cup or bowl, made of wood, simple enough to be present in this upper room, but special enough to be seen as worthy of the task.

The cup taken from the room of the Last Supper would later be used for its newly assigned purpose after the crucifixion. As one of the only women usually depicted standing at the foot of the cross, Mary would have been present to collect the blood that fell on the ground both as Christ hung crucified and as He was taken to the tomb, in accordance to the Hebrew tradition. However, this was not the only vessel that caught the flowing blood of Christ. There was another cup, belonging to Joseph of Arimathea, that was used inside the tomb during the preparation of Christ's body.

In learning about the Santo Cáliz of Valencia, it was discovered that the actual relic, the upper cup made of reddish-brown agate, was said to have come from Egypt. This information certainly lends itself to the assessment that it belonged, not to an ordinary person living during this time, but to a more wealthy, more widely traveled individual. The Bible describes Joseph of Arimathea as being a wealthy man, willing to give his own "new tomb" to the slain Christ. He also gave his funeral shroud, said to be the Shroud of Turin, for Christ's burial. The weave of this shroud is quite tight and fine in a pattern uncommon to Palestine, but closely resembling the weave used in Egypt in the linen wrappings for their mummified dead.

These pointers to Egypt indicate that both the Shroud and the cup atop the Santo Cáliz of Valencia were intended for use in Joseph's own fine burial. Therefore it is likely that Joseph of Arimathea used these items during the preparation of Christ's body before entombment. It should be remembered that Jesus was removed from the cross quickly, surprising Pilate that He was "already dead." The hasty removal of the body from the cross allowed the issuance of blood during the preparation in the tomb. This blood would have been gathered in something, according to Hebrew tradition. If Joseph used these funerary items to prepare Christ's body for the tomb, the rich agate cup of the Santo Cáliz would have been used for the purpose of catching any blood flowing from the body, just as it would have been used for Joseph's own burial.

When the preparations for Christ's entombment were complete, and the body wrapped in the shroud, the two containers used for the blood collection were left among the other items of the burial. Two days later, the tomb was discovered open and empty except for these grave items. When the followers of Jesus came to see the tomb, they feared for the body of their dead Lord, assuming it had been removed by the Romans for desecration. However in the days that followed,

Christ reappeared to them in His radiant resurrected form to reveal to them His divine nature, thus making these grave goods sacred objects.

It was at this point that several legends were born. The burial cloth was removed and maintained as a sacred relic since the image of Jesus was imprinted on the fabric. The legends of the Lance of Longinus, the True Cross, etc., would also be started by the objects left in the tomb for Empress Helena Augusta to discover later in the fourth century. Most importantly, the legend of the Holy Grail also began at this point.

Among those who revisited the tomb after the resurrected Christ had appeared were Saint Peter and the three people who played the largest part of His entombment. Saint Peter took from the tomb the most holy of the funerary objects left behind—the Santo Cáliz, the cup containing the pure blood of Christ. From this cup, he gave Joseph, Nicodemus, and Mary each a small amount of the blood in the five remaining alabastrons that Mary brought to the tomb to complete the ritual act of annointing.

Joseph and Nicodemus were given two samples each, and Mary appears to have been given only one since she had already used one to anoint Christ's feet when He attended a feast at her family's house. Saint Peter then took the reddish-brown cup of the Santo Cáliz with him in his journies to other lands to spread the teaching of Jesus. The other three took with them their share of the blood relics—Joseph and Mary journeyed together to France where Mary remained while Joseph continued to Britain, and Nicodemus chose to remain in Palestine, incorporating his vials of blood in his carving of Jesus, the Volto Santo. This would account for the five small vials that are among our most likely candidates for being associated with the Grail legend.

This leaves behind the last of the cups discussed previously—the Nanteos Cup. Why this cup was left behind when the Santo Cáliz was taken is a matter of conjecture. It may be that this cup containing Christ's blood was seen as less appealing as a sacred relic since the blood was mixed with dirt. It could also be a simple act of devotion in the Hebrew tradition—leaving behind some of the blood in the tomb. For whatever reason it was left behind, this idea is actually somewhat substantiated by the findings of Drs. Mary and Alan Whanger during their research of the Shroud of Turin. They have found what appears to be a blood stain on the cloth outside the areas where the body or any of the other objects would have been. It also appears that there is a scoop or a spoon projecting from this object imprinted on the shroud. It is possible that this is the container full of the bloody dirt that was collected by Mary at the foot of the cross.

Then in the fourth century, Empress Helena discovered the tomb, finding all the items included in Christ's burial inside. Among these objects was the small cup left behind—the Marian Chalice. While Graham Phillips believes this chalice is the onyx vial found in Hawstone Park, it is unlikely that a Roman Emperor, his Roman mother, or a later Greek historian would refer to this small vial as a "chalice." It would be clear to anyone at the time that this object would not be suitable as a drinking vessel but would be more suited for use as a container for oils, cosmetic pigments, or perfume. Therefore, if Olympiodorus had referred to the "Unguent Flask of Mary" or something similar, Phillips's conclusion would be much more likely.

There is another vessel among the possible Grails that matches both the description and the history of Olympiodorus's Marian Chalice much better than the Hawstone Park vial. The Nanteos Cup most closely fits the previous description of the vessel taken from the upper room of the Last Supper that Mary used in Christ's preparation. If one were to look at this wooden cup and the green onyx vial found in Hawstone Park, one would clearly choose the Nanteos Cup to be described as a chalice—the Marian Chalice.

Although this is a reasonable assumption, the most decisive factor of this theory is again in relation to Olympiodorus and his account of the Marian Chalice being sent to Britain for safety during the attacks on Rome around AD 410. It has been demonstrated how this sacred relic would have gone to Glastonbury, a center for Christian devotion and a place known to house other blood relics, rather than to a fortified Roman city. Since the Nanteos Cup was allegedly found hidden in the walls at Glastonbury Abbey before its removal to Strata Florida, and then to Nanteos Manor, the Marian Chalice mentioned by Olympiodorus must be the Nanteos Cup itself.

One may now wonder if the Nanteos Cup might be the original cup brought to Britain by Joseph of Arimathea. The tradition of Joseph coming to Britain is commonly thought to include a cup that he brought with him on his trip from Palestine; however, this was not the case. The earliest records and depictions of Joseph arriving at Glastonbury show him carrying two small cruets or jars, as previously described, which are rounded with a flared base and lip. Both the vials found in Hawstone Park and in Italy match this description perfectly. Although little is known of the alabaster jar found with Mary in her tomb or the original vials of blood found in the Volto Santo, they presumably had the same general characteristics.

This leads to the three characters of the Grail legend—Joseph, Nicodemus, and Mary Magdalene. Since the onyx vial was found in Shropshire, near both Glastonbury and the Nanteos Manor in Wales, it is quite likely that this vial once did in fact contain a blood relic of Jesus Christ, just as Graham Phillips stated. However, other vial relics associated with Mary and Nicodemus would indicate that this vial was one of the two brought to Britain by Joseph after being given the blood relic by Peter from the Santo Cáliz, not the Marian Chalice as Mr. Phillips thought.

This accounts for only one of Joseph's two vials that were brought from Palestine. It is possible that the other vial once belonging to Joseph of Arimathea now rests in the hands of Rocco Zingaro in Italy. If Joseph's relics were separated and sent to various locations, as reflected by the Grail text *Perlesvaus*, one of them might have ended up at Rosslyn Chapel in Scotland, a haven for refugee Templars after the dissolution of their order. If that were the case, it would stand to reason that the remnants of the modern-day Knights Templar would have it in their possession. Although it is made of glass instead of onyx as is the Hawstone Park vial, it is by no means certain that all the unguent flasks taken by Joseph, Mary, and Nicodemus were made of the same material. All that is known is that onyx, alabaster, and glass were materials available to each during the time of Christ, and were used in the production of alabastrons.

Now that all of the relics that can be justifiably called Holy Grail have been identified, the question must now be asked, how did these seven separate objects become combined into the one object described in the traditional Grail legend? To answer that question, one must begin again with Joseph and work backwards to the "originating" cup, the Santo Cáliz of Valencia.

Joseph did indeed start the Grail tradition in coming to Britain with relics of Christ's blood. He carried his two flasks to the peninsula of Glastonbury where he and his small band of followers built the early wattle church on the ruined site of the Lady Chapel at Glastonbury Abbey. Here Joseph began a quiet ecclesiastical tradition, with the two vials of Christ's blood at the center of their worship. Having similar vials containing blood relics of their own, Mary settled in France, away from Joseph, to live and die in relative obscurity, while Nicodemus hid his relics away in the Volto Santo. Although his carving of Christ did make its way into the Grail legend, it did so only in a slight and inconspicuous fashion. It was therefore Joseph of Arimathea at Glastonbury and his tradition there that laid the foundation for the more elaborate mystery that followed.

This tradition served as a determining factor when the decision was made to send the Marian Chalice, or Nanteos Cup, to Britain for safekeeping. It is interesting to note that the renowned King Arthur made his mark on history at the end of the fifth century AD, mere decades after the Nanteos Cup was sent to Glastonbury from Rome in AD 410. This is not to say that the historical King Arthur played any significant part in the history of the Nanteos Cup at Glastonbury, or that he ever saw it there at all. However it is noteworthy that King Arthur was taken to "Avalon," a name closely ascribed to Glastonbury at the center of the British marches, to be healed of his wounds and perhaps return again another day as king. It is likely that the fame of the Nanteos Cup and its alleged healing powers had already spread during the time of Arthur, and that he was taken to Glastonbury in the hope that he could be healed by it. It would be for this reason that Arthur became so closely associated with the Grail Quest.

It may also be due to the vials and the Nanteos Cup that a rift was formed between the religious center at Glastonbury and the Papacy in Rome.

> From Vatican records we know that during the early fifth century the Church in Britain was preaching an alternative apostolic succession. Known as Pelagianism (after one of its exponents, Pelagius), it dared to question the authority of the Roman popes. Although most records of doctrine were destroyed, it is possible that the Pelagians believed that their succession descended from Joseph of Arimathea [Phillips, p. 53].

This clash would have been caused by the idea that both churches, that at Glastonbury and that in Rome, were founded from the very blood of Christ—the Holy Grail.

In the history of the Santo Cáliz, we also see a connection between the Grail and the Knights Templar. In the earlier description of the Santo Cáliz during its time at the monastary of San Juan de la Peña, we learned that Don Alfonso the Battler, who gave his kingdom to the Knights Templar after his death, made his "proto-Templar" knights swear an oath of loyalty before the Santo Cáliz. It is likely that the Templars either simply perpetuated this tradition in their own practice, or the tradition was assigned to them later by the writers of the Grail texts.

Spain also offers one possible link to the "source book" which Chrétien was given before he began to write his Grail text. Wolfram von Eschenbach claims he used the same source book as that used by Chrétien, only he claims that his French counterpart did not do the original tale justice. He claims the source book was written by someone named Kyot.

> Toledo was one of the major centers of learning in Europe where Christian, Arab and Jewish scholars congregated—in the twelfth century there were 12,000 Jews in the city. Here Kyot learned the secrets of the Grail from Flegetanis, a baptized pagan astrologer of the race of Solomon, and passed them on to Wolfram von Eschenbach [Begg and Begg, p. 122].

Kyot has been identified as Guiot de Provence, who was said to be a member of the Knights Templar in the Court of Frederick Barbarosa.

It is now clear that the Grail legend is not as simple as it once seemed. The historical Holy Grail is not one object to be found at the end of a long quest. It is a truth that demands a great deal of investigating and understanding. The Grail legend was built on the backs of several preexisting traditions, based on several very real artifacts. The True Grail, the Grail that is not only real but extraordinarily complex, can be outlined by examining the following table.

The Santo Cáliz of Valencia	Original funerary item placed in Christ's tomb for collection of blood (from body)	IS: Gold/Jeweled Cup described in Grail texts	IS NOT: Relic brought to Britain by Joseph
		Relic venerated by Knights Templar	Cup used at Last Supper
The Nanteos Cup	Original funerary item placed in Christ's tomb for collection of blood (spilled on the ground)	IS: Cup from Upper Room of Last Supper	IS NOT: Relic brought to Britain by Joseph
		Marian Chalice recorded by Olympiodorus	Gold/Jeweled Cup described in Grail texts

		IS:	
		Reason for King Arthur's association with Grail story	
		Likely reason for Grail being said to have healing properties	
Vials of Joseph Nicodemus, and and Mary Magdalene	Secondary, personal reliquaries, NOT placed in tomb	*ARE:* Relics Joseph brought to Britain	*ARE NOT:* Grail cups in traditional sense
		Relics found in Volto Santo	Cup used at Last Supper
		Alabaster Jar found with Mary's body	

Such is the nature of the True Grail. The Grail is not only a true, physical object, but the truth behind the legend has proven to be even stranger than the fiction written about it. In following the history and the leads available today, after almost two thousand years of mystery and retelling, the myth of the Grail as simply a spiritual or psychological abstraction has been shattered. The historical reference written by Olympiodorus has negated the assumption that the Grail was simply the magical cauldron of Celtic mythology rewritten to suit Christian themes. The relics associated with other saints, Joseph, Mary, and Nicodemus, have demonstrated the multiplicity of the historical Grail. The quiet valley in which Nanteos Manor rests has provided the link back to Glastonbury, and thus Olympiodorus, which explains the close relationship between Grail lore and Arthurian legend. Lastly, the Roman Catholic Church, which fought so long against the Grail and all of its heretical attributes, has provided the rich histories and traditions that point back to the Santo Cáliz of Valencia, the cup that began it all.

It is not easy to respect or accept the information presented herein. It goes against everything we have come to accept about the Grail. However, among all theories currently presented, this thesis both explains all of the lingering questions regarding the Grail and accounts for all historical and archeological evidence pertaining to the Grail legend.

Hindsight is always perfect, as the saying goes. However, the process that reaches that state of perfect vision is not instantaneous or in any way easy. The courage to question everything is the wheel against which the lenses of hindsight are ground. Accepting the unacceptable answers to questions you didn't know to ask is the quality which makes us human, and enables us to take the leaps of understanding, the leaps of faith, which grant wisdom.

In the end, the Grail riddle remains—What is the Grail? This riddle is unique among all other riddles in the sense that the question is the answer. All the Grail hero must do to achieve the Grail is to ask the question and inquire about the mysterious relic. Therefore, all who undertake the task of understanding the Grail immediately find what they are seeking.

Here, in this analysis of the historical Grail and its legends, a final truth has been achieved, not by digging through mounds of mystery until at last the golden idol of fact is uncovered. This conclusion was reached simply by always inquiring, questioning, and being willing to follow reason and logic wherever it may lead. This alone has allowed the realization that the real, true historical Grail is not the cup used by Christ at the Last Supper, and later passed to Joseph of Arimathea. It is a number of things, each lending a different color to the complex tapestry upon which is woven the Grail legend, hanging illuminated as a beacon to the future seekers of truth.

BIBLIOGRAPHY

Ashe, Geoffrey. *The Discovery of King Arthur.* New York: Henry Holt and Company, 1985.

Baigent, Michael, Richard Leigh, and Henry Lincoln. *Holy Blood, Holy Grail.* New York: Dell Publishing, 1983.

Begg, Ean, and Deike Begg. *In Search of the Holy Grail and the Precious Blood.* London: Thorsons, 1995.

Bliss, Geoffrey, and Rose Bliss. *Nanteos Manor Guide Book.* Aberystwyth, Wales: The Cambrian News Ltd.

Cameron, Ron. *The Other Gospels: Non-Canonical Gospel Texts.* Philadelphia: The Westminster Press, 1982.

Capt, E. Raymond. *The Traditions of Glastonbury.* Thousand Oaks, Calif.: Artisan Sales, 1983.

Carley, James P. *The Chronicle of Glastonbury Abbey: An Edition, Translation and Study of John of Glastonbury's Cronica Sive Antiquitates Glastoniensis Ecclesie.* Woodbridge, Suffolk: The Boydell Press, 1985.

_____. *Glastonbury Abbey: The Holy House at the Head of the Moors Adventurous.* New York: St. Martin's Press, 1988.

Central Somerset Gazette Official Guide to Glastonbury. Glastonbury: Avalon Press, 1923.

Chrétien de Troyes. *Perceval: Or the Story of the Grail.* Ruth Harwood Cline, trans. Athens: University of Georgia Press, 1985.

Coghlan, Ronan. *The Illustrated Encyclopedia of Arthurian Legends.* New York: Barnes and Noble Books, 1995.

Cruz, Joan Carroll. *Relics.* Indiana: Our Sunday Visitor, Inc., 1984.

Drijvers, Jan Willem. *Helena Augusta: The Mother of Constantine the Great and the Legend of Her Finding of the True Cross.* New York: Brill's Studies in Intellectual History, 1992.

Fleming, Stuart J. *Roman Glass: Reflections on Cultural Change.* Philadelphia: University of Pennsylvania Museum of Archaeology and Anthropology, 1999.

Gilbert, Adrian. *The Holy Kingdom.* London: Bantam Press, 1998.

Godwin, Malcolm. *The Holy Grail: Its Origins, Secrets, & Meaning Revealed.* New York: Viking Studio Books, 1994.

Goodrich, Norma Lorre. *The Holy Grail.* New York: HarperCollins Publishers, 1992.

The Holy Bible. (KJV and NIV.)

Illustrated Dictionary of Bible Life and Times. New York: The Reader's Digest Association, Inc., 1989.

Lazzarini, Pietro. *Il Volto Santo di Lucca.* Lucca, Italy: C. Carolus Pezzini Vic. Gen., 1980.

Loomis, Roger Sherman. *The Grail: From Celtic Myth to Christian Symbol.* Princeton, N.J.: Princeton University Press, 1991.

The Mabinogion. Translated by Lady Charlotte E. Guest. New York: Dover Publications, Inc., 1997.

Matthews, John. *The Elements of the Grail Tradition.* Shaftesbury, Dorset: Element Books Limited, 1990.

McKay, John P., Bennett D. Hill, and John Buckler. *A History of Western Society: Fourth Edition.* Boston: Houghton Mifflin Company, 1991.

Navarrete, Manuel Sanchez. *El Santo Cáliz de la Cena.* Valencia: Cofradia del Santo Cáliz, 1994.

Phillips, Graham. *The Search for the Grail.* London: Century, 1995.

Ravenscroft, Trevor. *The Spear of Destiny.* York Beach, Maine: Samuel Weiser, Inc., 1982.

Reader's Digest Atlas of the Bible: An Illustrated Guide to the Holy Land. New York: The Reader's Digest Association, Inc., 1981.

Sinclair, Andrew. *The Sword and the Grail: Of the Grail and the Templars and a True Discovery of America.* New York: Crown Publishers, Inc., 1992.

Staines, David. *The Complete Romances of Chrétien de Troyes.* Bloomington: Indiana University Press, 1990.

Starbird, Margaret. *The Woman with the Alabaster Jar.* Santa Fe, New Mexico: Bear & Company Publishing, 1993.

Tate, Georges. *The Crusaders: Warriors of God.* London: Harry N. Abrams, Inc., 1996.

Westwood, Jennifer. *Mysterious Places: The World's Unexplained Symbolic Sites, Ancient Cities, and Lost Lands.* New York: Galahad Books, 1987.

Whanger, Mary, and Alan Whanger. *The Shroud of Turin: An Adventure of Discovery.* Franklin, Tenn.: Providence House Publishers, 1998.

Wilhelm, James J. *The Romance of Arthur: An Anthology of Medieval Texts in Translation.* New York: Garland Publishing, Inc., 1994.

INDEX